Key Stage 2

Science Revision Guide

Penny Johnson

Schofield & Sims

Welcome to this book

This book will help you revise the science you have learnt in Key Stage 2.

Green headings show you which topic is covered.

This tells you where to look for more information.

Find out about words in **bold** by turning to the Glossary.

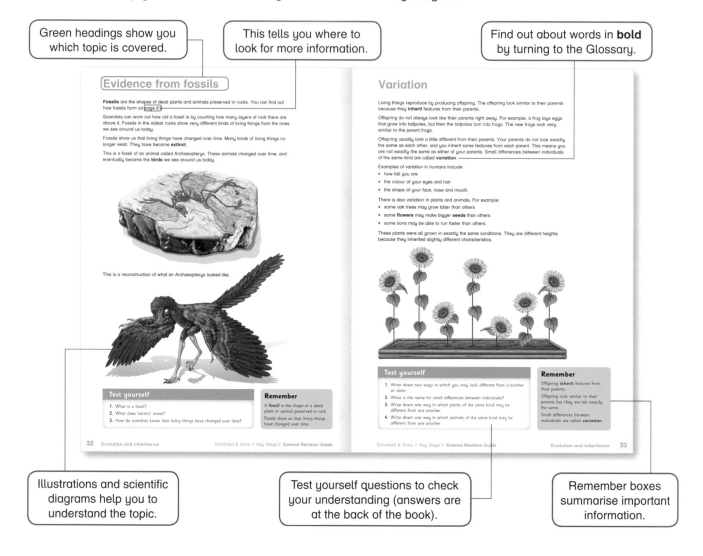

Illustrations and scientific diagrams help you to understand the topic.

Test yourself questions to check your understanding (answers are at the back of the book).

Remember boxes summarise important information.

How to revise

- Turn to the topic and read about it.
- Read the Remember box and then cover it up. Can you remember what it says?
- Read the Test yourself questions and write your answers on a piece of paper.
- Check your answers against the right answers at the back of the book.
- If you got any answers wrong, read the topic again and have another go at the questions.
- If you got the answers right – well done! Move on to the next topic.
- Once you have worked through this revision guide, move on to the **Key Stage 2 Science Practice Papers**.

Tips for tests

- Always read the question carefully before you answer it.
- Have a go at as many questions as you can. If there is a question you really can't answer, just move on to the next one. You can always come back to it if you have time.
- If you are asked to explain something, you have to give a reason why it happens.
- Use scientific words if you can. For example, 'transparent' instead of 'see-through'.
- If you have time at the end, check through your work.

Contents

Plant parts

Plants are very important to us because they provide us with food. We eat some plants directly, such as peas or apples. When we eat meat, we are eating an animal that has fed on plants.

Plants are living things. They have different parts and all the parts need to work together to keep the plant healthy. Plants need light, air, water and warmth. Plants do not move around like animals, but they can move parts of themselves.

Parts of a plant

The **flowers** help the plant to reproduce. You will learn more about flowers and **reproduction** on pages 6 to 8.

Plants make food using their **leaves**. The leaves need light, air, water and warmth to make food.

The **stem** supports the plant. The stem has little tubes inside it. Water can travel up these tubes to reach the leaves. The 'stem' of a tree is called a **trunk**.

The **roots** hold the plant in the **soil** and take in water from it.

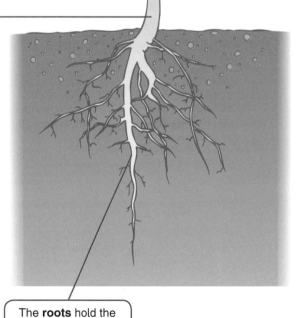

Remember

Plants need light, air, water and warmth to grow well.

Plants make food using their **leaves**.

Stems support the plant and take water up to the leaves.

Roots hold the plant in the **soil** and take in water.

All the parts of a plant need to work together.

Test yourself

1. Why do plants need leaves?
2. Why do plants need stems?
3. Why do plants need roots?
4. Look at these two plants.

A

B

a Which plant will grow well?
b Explain your answer.

Growing plants

Plants need light, air, water and warmth to grow well. Plants also need room to grow. Plants make new materials to help them grow using water, air and light. The new materials are made in the leaves. The process of making food in the leaves is called **photosynthesis**.

Plants also need small amounts of other substances to keep them healthy. These nutrients **dissolve** in water in the soil and are taken in through the roots. If there are not enough **nutrients** in the soil to keep plants healthy, a farmer or a gardener might add **fertiliser**. The fertiliser adds nutrients to the soil. Some bottles of fertiliser for house plants say 'plant food' on the label. This is not correct scientifically! Remember that plants make their own food in their leaves.

Different plants grow best in different soils, as you will see from the examples below.

Different plants, different needs

Marram grass grows on sand dunes, where there is not much water.

Bogbean plants grow in very wet places.

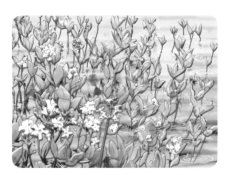

Different plants have different kinds of roots. This oak tree is very tall and its roots spread out a long way. The roots need to be strong to support the tree in windy weather. All the little 'branches' in the roots help the tree to take in water.

This carrot plant does not need deep roots, because it is only a small plant and the wind cannot blow it over. The thick part of the root stores food.

Remember

Plants make new materials from water, air and light.

Plants take in water through their **roots**. Plants also take in **nutrients** through their roots, which they need to keep healthy.

Different plants grow best in different **soils**.

Test yourself

1. What do plants need to make their own food?

2. Write down two things that plants take in through their roots.

3. Why do gardeners sometimes add fertiliser to the soil?

4. Why do tall trees need deeper roots than small plants?

5. What kind of roots do you think grass plants have? Explain your answer.

Flowers and reproduction

Plants reproduce (make new plants like themselves) by making **seeds**. The process of **reproduction** in plants is described in the diagram below. There are several stages in the **life cycle** of plants. You will find out more about the different stages on pages 7 to 8.

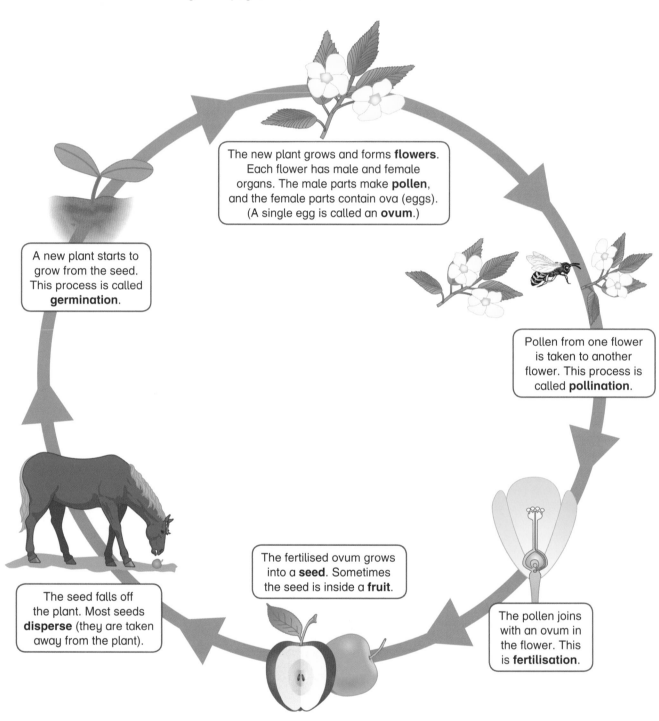

The new plant grows and forms **flowers**. Each flower has male and female organs. The male parts make **pollen**, and the female parts contain ova (eggs). (A single egg is called an **ovum**.)

A new plant starts to grow from the seed. This process is called **germination**.

Pollen from one flower is taken to another flower. This process is called **pollination**.

The fertilised ovum grows into a **seed**. Sometimes the seed is inside a **fruit**.

The seed falls off the plant. Most seeds **disperse** (they are taken away from the plant).

The pollen joins with an ovum in the flower. This is **fertilisation**.

Test yourself

1. What happens during pollination?
2. What happens during fertilisation?
3. What does 'seed dispersal' mean?
4. What happens during germination?

Remember

Plants reproduce by making **seeds**.

There are several stages in the **life cycle** of a plant.

Pollination and fertilisation

Pollination

Pollen from flowers has to be carried to other flowers for plants to reproduce. This is pollination. It is an important part of the reproduction process. Pollen can be carried by insects or by the wind.

Some flowers make a sweet **liquid** called **nectar** that insects feed on. Pollen gets on to insects when they crawl inside the flower to get the nectar. The pollen is brushed off on to the **stigma** of the next flower the insects visit.

Flowers that are pollinated by insects usually have bright and colourful **petals**. These act like a signal to insects, to attract them to the nectar.

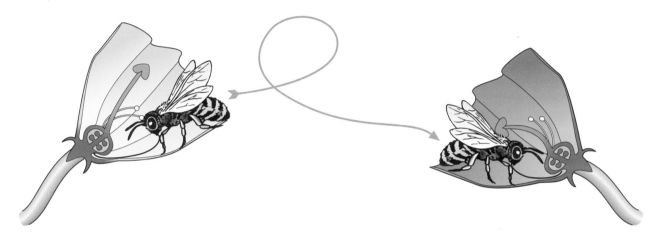

Did you know that grass has flowers? Grass pollen is carried from one plant to another by the wind, so the pollen grains are very small and light. The flowers do not need to attract insects, so they do not need to be large and colourful.

Remember

Pollen can be transferred from one **flower** to another by insects or by the wind.

Pollen lands on the **stigma** and a tube grows down the **style**.

Fertilisation happens when the pollen grain joins an **ovum**.

The fertilised ovum grows into a **seed**.

Fertilisation

When pollen lands on the stigma of a flower, it starts to grow a little tube down the **style**. The pollen grain travels down this tube and joins an ovum. This is called fertilisation. When an ovum has been fertilised, it starts to grow into a seed. The **ovary** grows into a fruit.

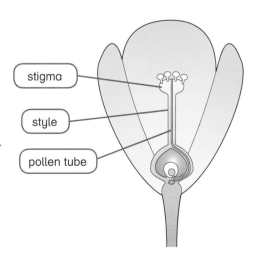

stigma

style

pollen tube

Test yourself

1. Why do some flowers have brightly coloured petals?
2. Why do some flowers make nectar?
3. What does a fertilised ovum change into?
4. Explain the difference between pollination and fertilisation.

Seed dispersal

After **fertilisation**, a fertilised **ovum** will grow into a **seed**. When the seeds are ready, they fall off the plant and may start to grow into new plants.

If all the seeds landed around the parent plant they would be too crowded. They would not have enough space to grow and they would not get enough light, air, water or **nutrients**. The seeds have to **disperse** (be spread out) so that they have room to grow.

The wind carries some seeds away from the parent plant. Seeds that are carried by the wind are light and fluffy or have 'wings'.

dandelion seeds   sycamore seed

Water disperses some seeds. For example, coconuts often land in the sea and are carried away from the parent tree.

Some seeds are dispersed by explosion. Lupin seeds grow in pods. When the seeds are ready the pod splits open suddenly and the seeds are flung away.

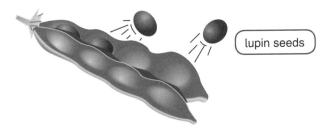

lupin seeds

Animals disperse seeds. Apple seeds ('pips') are inside a juicy **fruit**. Animals eat the fruit and the seeds inside pass right through their bodies and come out in their droppings.

Animals can also spread some seeds by carrying them around on their fur. Burdock seeds are covered in tiny hooks, which catch on fur.

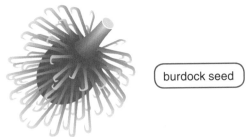

burdock seed

Test yourself

1. Why do seeds need to be dispersed?
2. Write down four ways that seeds can be dispersed.
3. Why are dandelion seeds light and fluffy?
4. Why do some seeds have a juicy fruit around them?

Remember

Seeds need to be dispersed to get enough space, light, air, water and **nutrients** to grow.

Seeds can be dispersed by wind, water, animals or by explosion.

Shapes and functions

Different parts of plants have different shapes and structures depending on their **function** (the job they do).

- Plant **stems** have tubes inside them to carry water and they are stiff so they can support the plant.
- **Roots** split up into smaller and smaller 'branches' so they can spread out in the **soil** and absorb water. This also helps them to hold the plant in the soil.
- **Leaves** are flat so they have a large area to absorb light.
- **Petals** are often coloured to attract insects for **pollination**.

Water transport experiment

Ruby and Amir have different ideas about how water travels through a plant.

Ruby thinks that water travels from the roots to all parts of the plant in little tubes inside the plant.

Amir thinks that water travels up through *all* of the stem.

Ruby and Amir used a celery stick and a carnation **flower**. They put them both into beakers with coloured water.

After a few hours, they took the celery out and cut through the stem. This is what they saw.

This is what the petals of the carnation flower looked like.

The results of the experiment show that Ruby was right. Water travels through a plant in little tubes inside the plant.

Test yourself

1. Write down two functions of the stem of a plant.
2. How does the stem transport water to the leaves?
3. Look at the result of Ruby and Amir's experiment. Explain how their results show that Ruby was right.
4. Explain how the shape of the roots of a plant help the roots to carry out their functions.

Remember

Different parts of plants have different **functions** (jobs).

The shapes and structures of plant parts depend on their functions.

Water travels through plants in little tubes.

Sorting out living things

There are millions of different kinds of living things. It is very difficult to think about all these things separately, so scientists put them into groups. All the living things in a group are similar in some way.

The two main groups of living things are animals and plants. There are many differences between animals and plants, but the main difference is that plants can make their own food. Animals cannot do this – they have to eat plants or other animals for their food.

Animals are divided into smaller groups. One group contains all the animals that have backbones – this group includes humans. These animals are called **vertebrates**. Animals that do not have backbones are called **invertebrates**. The vertebrates are divided into five smaller groups, called **amphibians**, **birds**, **fish**, **mammals** and **reptiles**.

You can use a **key** to help you to work out which group something belongs to. Start at the top and answer each question. The blue line on the key shows you how to work out which group you belong to!

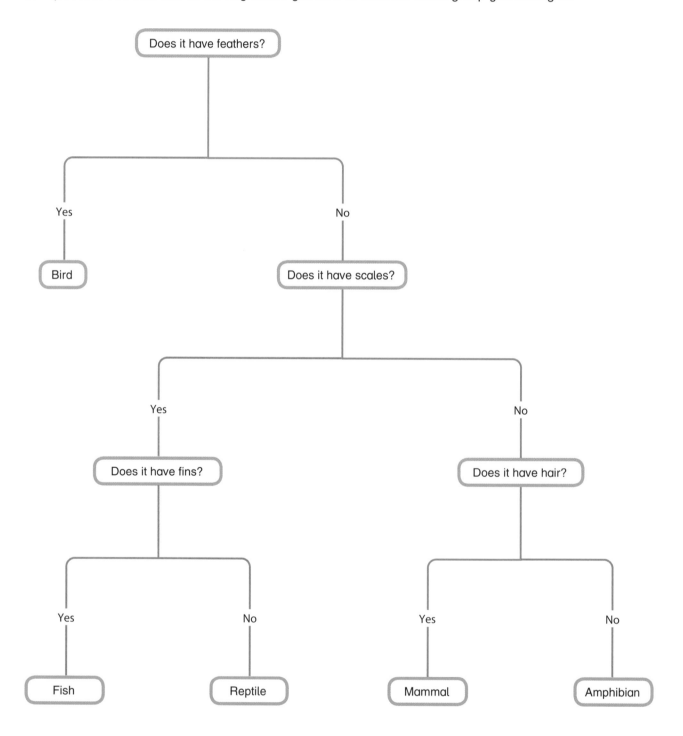

Looking at seabirds

Here is another key, similar to the one on page 10. This key helps you to identify some birds that live near the sea.

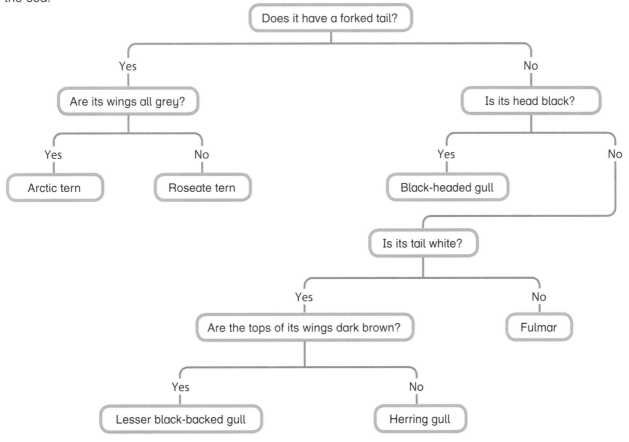

The example below shows you how the key can be used.

What is this bird?

You can use the key above to help you to identify this bird.

These are the answers to all the questions for this bird.

Does it have a forked tail?   *No*

Is its head black?   *No*

Is its tail white?   *Yes*

Are the tops of its wings dark brown?   *No*

Answer *It is a herring gull.*

Test yourself

1. Why do scientists put living things into groups?
2. What is the main difference between animals and plants?
3. Use the key on this page to identify these seabirds.

a   b   c   d

Remember

Scientists put living things into groups to make studying them easier.

The two main groups are animals and plants.

We can use **keys** to help us to identify living things.

More on classification

On page 10 you saw that all living things can be divided into groups. The main groups are plants and animals. **Micro-organisms** are living things that are too small to see unless you use a microscope. Some of these are plants, but most have their own group. These include **fungi** and **bacteria**.

Plants

Plants can be divided up into groups. The main group of plants is the **flowering plants**. This group includes grasses and most trees. Other groups are **conifers** and **mosses**.

> Many conifers have needle-shaped **leaves** and have **seeds** that form in cones.

Vertebrates

You read on page 10 that animals can be divided into **vertebrates** and **invertebrates**. Each group of vertebrates has several things in common.

Birds all have feathers and lay eggs with hard shells.

Fish all have wet scales and lay eggs in water.

Reptiles all have dry scales and lay eggs with leathery shells.

Mammals all have hair, produce milk and give birth to live young.

Amphibians all have moist skin and lay eggs in water.

Invertebrates

Invertebrates can also be divided into groups.

Insects have six legs (in three pairs). Their bodies are divided into three parts. Many insects have wings.

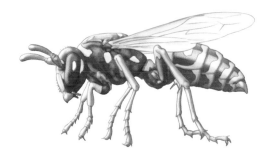

Spiders all have eight legs (in four pairs). Their bodies are divided into two sections. They do not have wings.

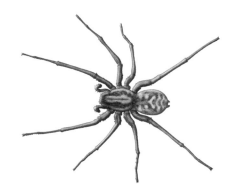

The group of **molluscs** includes snails. Many molluscs have shells.

Worms have no hard parts and no legs.

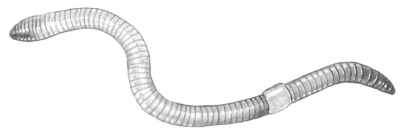

Remember

Micro-organisms are too small to see unless you use a microscope.

The group 'plants' can be divided into smaller groups. Some of these are **flowering plants**, **conifers** and **mosses**.

Invertebrates can be divided into smaller groups. Some of these are insects, spiders, **molluscs** and worms.

Test yourself

1. Dogs and humans are both mammals. What features do they have in common?
2. Write down two things that all fish have in common.
3. A bee is an insect. How many legs does it have?
4. A small animal has eight legs. Do you think it has wings? Explain your answer.

Environments and habitats

All living organisms live somewhere. The place where an organism lives is its **habitat**. The word **environment** means the conditions in a habitat. For example, some habitats are warm and some are cold. Some habitats are shady and some get lots of sunshine.

A woodland habitat

This is a woodland habitat. Rabbits, squirrels and birds live here. The woodland is also the habitat for insects, worms, grass, trees and bushes.

The habitat provides food for the organisms that live there. The rabbit eats grass, the squirrel eats acorns and other nuts and the fox eats rabbits!

The conditions in a habitat change during the year. In the woodland, most of the trees will lose their **leaves** during the winter and the weather will be much colder and wetter than in the summer. There is not as much food in the winter and so some animals may die.

Environments can change for other reasons, too. For example, humans could cut down some of the trees. This would affect animals that need those trees for food or shelter.

Different organisms need each other

The animals and plants in a habitat all need each other. Some animals need the plants for food.

Nutrients in the plants get back into the **soil** in the animals' droppings, so the plants need the animals, too. Some plants need insects to pollinate them.

A pond habitat

This is a pond habitat. The conditions here are different from the conditions in a woodland, so different organisms live here.

Humans can affect many environments. The environment in a pond may be changed if chemicals that farmers put on their fields run into the water. The chemicals may kill some of the things that live there.

Humans can also help to improve environments. Sometimes one kind of plant grows too quickly and other things cannot grow there. Humans can help to keep the environment fit for many different things to live there.

Micro-habitats

Some habitats can be quite small. A flower bed is a habitat. Even the little patch of soil underneath a stone can be a habitat and may support hundreds of tiny creatures. A very small habitat like this is called a **micro-habitat**.

Test yourself

1. What is a habitat?
2. **a** Make a list of the organisms that live in a woodland habitat.
   b Make a list of the organisms that live in a pond habitat.
3. Write down two ways in which humans can affect a habitat.
4. Which organisms do you think you would find living in a habitat under a stone?

Remember

A **habitat** is the place where an organism lives.

The plants and animals in a habitat need each other.

Plants and animals are **adapted** to help them to live in their habitat.

Different life cycles

The **life cycle** of an animal describes how it reproduces and what happens to the young until they are ready to reproduce themselves.

Mammal life cycles

Humans are **mammals**. A human baby grows inside its mother for nine months before it is born. When it is small, a baby can be fed milk made by its mother. A human child needs to be looked after for many years before it is old enough to have babies of its own.

The life cycles of other mammals are similar, but may take different times. A baby elephant grows inside its mother for nearly two years before it is born. A mother elephant usually only has one baby at a time. A mother cat can have up to ten kittens at once and they only grow inside her for about two months.

Bird life cycles

Baby **birds** hatch from eggs. The egg contains food for the growing baby bird. The parent birds must keep their eggs warm, which they do by sitting on the nest. The baby birds need to be fed by their parents until they have grown enough to be able to fly and find food for themselves.

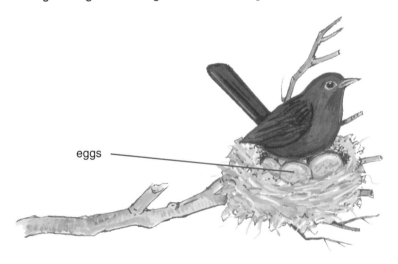

eggs

Baby mammals usually look very similar to their parents. Baby birds, however, do not look quite like their parents because they have fluffy feathers, but they are the same basic shapes. Some other groups of animals have young that look completely different from the adults.

Amphibian life cycles

Here is the life cycle of a frog.

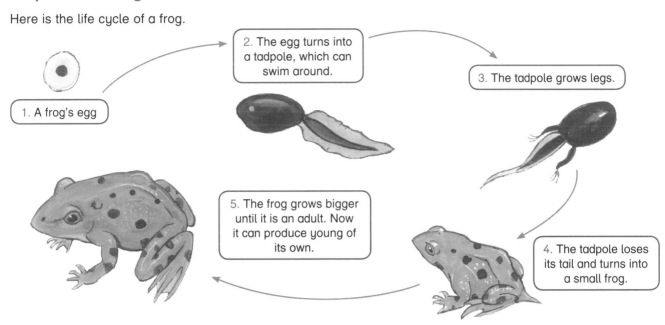

Tadpoles live in water and eat mostly tiny water plants. They will not survive if they are taken out of the water. Frogs can survive underwater and on land, although they need to keep their skin moist. The life cycles of other **amphibians** are similar.

Insect life cycles

Here is the life cycle of a butterfly.

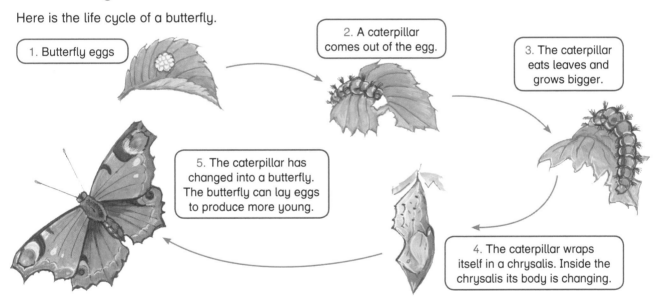

The life cycles of other insects are similar. Flies lay eggs on dead animals and the maggots eat the rotting meat until they are ready to turn into the adult form.

Test yourself

1. Write down three animal groups that lay eggs.
2. Write down two animal groups where the babies look similar to the adults.
3. Which animal group has young that can only live underwater at first?
4. Write down two ways in which the life cycles of amphibians and insects are similar and one way in which they are different.

Remember

A **life cycle** describes how an animal is born and grows up until it is ready to reproduce. Baby **mammals** grow inside their mothers, baby **birds** grow inside eggs. Young insects and **amphibians** look very different from their parents at first.

Sexual and asexual reproduction

Sexual reproduction in plants

Page 6 shows the **life cycle** of a plant. This is **sexual reproduction** because the plant cannot make **seeds** until **pollen** from the male organs of a **flower** combine with an **ovum** (egg) from the female part of another flower. This happens during **pollination** and **fertilisation**.

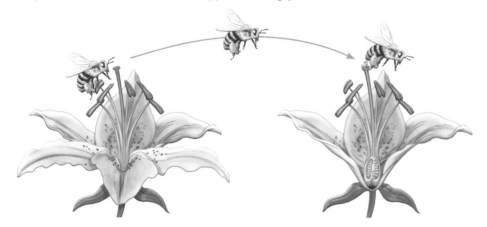

The offspring produced by sexual reproduction may have some characteristics of each of the parent flowers.

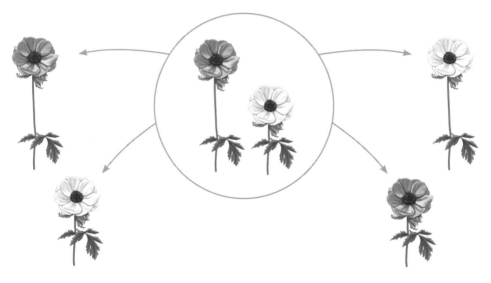

Asexual reproduction in plants

Plants can reproduce by **asexual reproduction** as well as by sexual reproduction. This is when there is only one parent plant. The offspring are identical to the parents.

Daffodils and other plants that grow from bulbs can reproduce asexually by splitting the bulb, found underground. Each part of the split bulb grows into a separate plant.

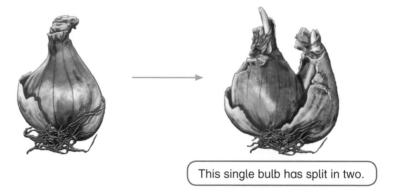

This single bulb has split in two.

Some plants send out plantlets on long **stems**. If these plantlets touch the **soil**, they can grow **roots** of their own and grow into new plants.

Plantlets

Spider plants produce plantlets.

Humans can also make plants reproduce asexually by taking **cuttings**. Parts of the stem of a plant are cut off and each part is put into soil, kept warm and given plenty of water. Each part of the stem will grow into a new plant.

Reproduction in animals

Most animals only reproduce by sexual reproduction. The male animal produces **sperm**. The female animal produces one or more eggs. The sperm fertilise the eggs when the animals mate.

Just like sexual reproduction in plants, the offspring of sexual reproduction in animals can have characteristics of both parents.

A few animals can reproduce both sexually and asexually. Greenfly are insects that attack rose bushes. They reproduce asexually for most of the year.

Test yourself

1. What joins up during fertilisation in plants?
2. What joins up during fertilisation in animals?
3. A gardener buys 20 new plants that are all exactly the same as each other. Have they been produced by sexual or asexual reproduction?
4. Can you think of a reason asexual reproduction might help plants to produce more offspring?

Remember

Sexual reproduction requires a male and a female parent. Sexual reproduction happens in plants and animals.

Asexual reproduction only needs one parent. Most plants can reproduce asexually.

A healthy diet

Animals need to eat plants or other animals because they cannot make their own food. They get **nutrition** from what they eat.

Your **diet** is all the different kinds of food that you eat each day.

You need food to:

- help you grow
- keep your body healthy
- give you energy to move around.

You need different foods to help your body to do all of these things.

Foods to help you grow

- Meat and fish

- Milk, cheese and eggs

- Beans and lentils

Foods to keep your body healthy

- Fruit

- Vegetables

Foods to give you energy

- Bread, pasta, rice and cereals contain starch.

- Milk, cheese, butter, cooking oil and meat contain fats and oils. You should not eat too much of these foods.

- Sweets, cakes, biscuits and fizzy drinks contain sugar. You should not eat too much of these foods.

What is a balanced diet?

A diet that has the right **mixture** of different foods to give your body all that it needs is called a **balanced diet**.

You need:

- some food for growth

- more food for health

- even more food for energy
  – this should be mainly
  starchy foods such as
  bread, pasta and cereals.

There are lots of different ways of getting a balanced diet. These meals all give you the foods your body needs.

Chicken with vegetables   Spaghetti and salad   Stir-fried vegetables with rice

Animals also need healthy diets. Different animals need different diets. For example, pet rabbits need to eat a lot of leaves and vegetables such as carrots. Cats need to eat a lot of meat and fish.

Test yourself

1. Write down three reasons your body needs food.
2. Which foods help your body to grow?
3. Which foods give you energy?
4. Which foods keep your body healthy?
5. What is a balanced diet?
6. Mia eats fish and chips at lunchtime and has a burger in a bun for tea. Explain to Mia how and why she should change her diet.

Remember

A healthy **diet** gives you food for growth and for energy, and keeps your body healthy.

A **balanced diet** gives your body all the different kinds of foods that it needs.

Skeletons

You have a **skeleton** inside your body. Your skeleton is made of lots of different bones. Your bones were very small when you were born and they got bigger as you grew bigger.

Your skeleton does three jobs:

- it protects parts of your body
- it supports your body (you couldn't stand up without your skeleton!)
- it lets you move.

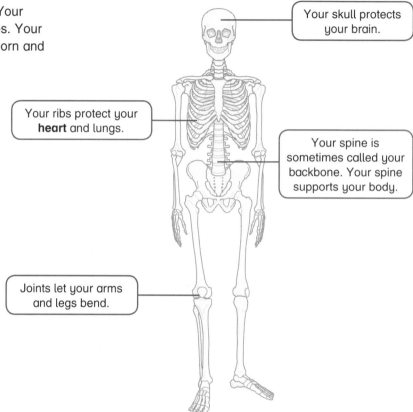

Your skull protects your brain.

Your ribs protect your **heart** and lungs.

Your spine is sometimes called your backbone. Your spine supports your body.

Joints let your arms and legs bend.

Do other animals have skeletons?

Many other animals have skeletons. All animals that have a spine are called **vertebrates**.

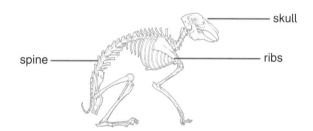

skull

spine

ribs

Some animals do not have skeletons. They are called **invertebrates**. Animals such as crabs have hard parts outside their bodies.

Animals such as worms do not have hard parts at all.

Test yourself

1. Write down three reasons you need a skeleton.
2. What does your skull do?
3. How does your skeleton allow you to move?

Remember

Your **skeleton** protects and supports your body and allows you to move.

Not all animals have a skeleton.

Muscles

The joints in your skeleton let your body move, but your bones cannot move on their own! You need **muscles** to move your arms and legs.

Muscles pull on your bones to move your body. When a muscle pulls, it contracts (gets shorter).

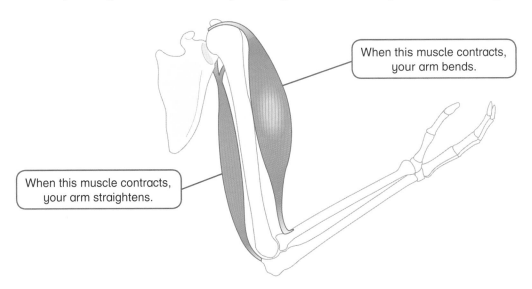

When this muscle contracts, your arm bends.

When this muscle contracts, your arm straightens.

Your muscles can only pull on bones. They cannot push. This means that your muscles have to work in pairs. When one muscle is contracting, the other is relaxing (getting longer).

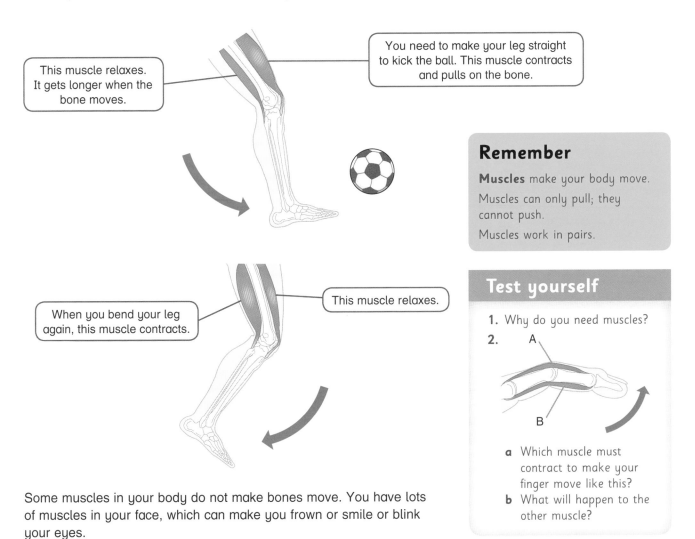

This muscle relaxes. It gets longer when the bone moves.

You need to make your leg straight to kick the ball. This muscle contracts and pulls on the bone.

When you bend your leg again, this muscle contracts.

This muscle relaxes.

Some muscles in your body do not make bones move. You have lots of muscles in your face, which can make you frown or smile or blink your eyes.

Test yourself

1. Why do you need muscles?

2. A

   B

   a Which muscle must contract to make your finger move like this?

   b What will happen to the other muscle?

Digestive system

The food you eat has to be broken down into simpler substances so that your body can absorb it and use it. This happens in your **digestive system**.

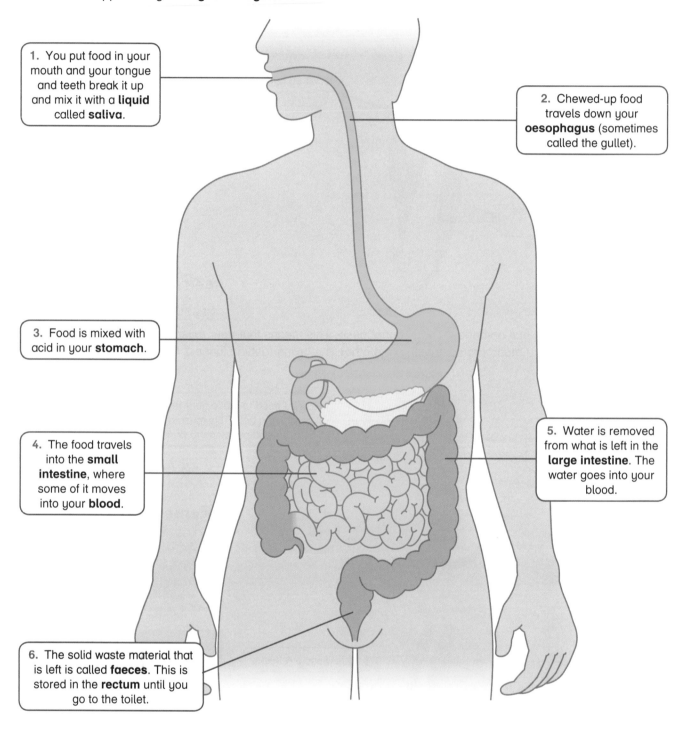

1. You put food in your mouth and your tongue and teeth break it up and mix it with a **liquid** called **saliva**.

2. Chewed-up food travels down your **oesophagus** (sometimes called the gullet).

3. Food is mixed with acid in your **stomach**.

4. The food travels into the **small intestine**, where some of it moves into your **blood**.

5. Water is removed from what is left in the **large intestine**. The water goes into your blood.

6. The solid waste material that is left is called **faeces**. This is stored in the **rectum** until you go to the toilet.

Test yourself

1. Where does your food get chopped up into smaller pieces?
2. Where do food substances get absorbed into your blood?
3. Write down two places in your digestive system where food gets mixed up with liquids.

Remember

Your **digestive system** breaks up food into simpler substances.

Food is chopped up and mixed with **saliva** in your mouth.

Food then goes to your **stomach** and your **small** and **large intestines**.

Teeth

You need teeth to help you eat. Your food needs to be cut into small pieces and chewed before you swallow it.

Your teeth have different shapes to do different jobs.

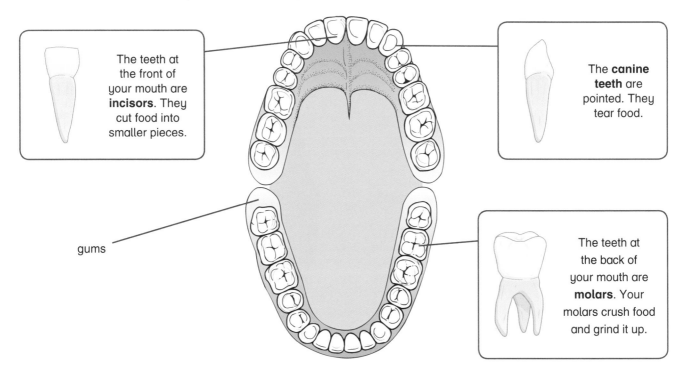

The teeth at the front of your mouth are **incisors**. They cut food into smaller pieces.

The **canine teeth** are pointed. They tear food.

gums

The teeth at the back of your mouth are **molars**. Your molars crush food and grind it up.

When you were born, you didn't have any teeth. Your first teeth are your milk teeth. They started to grow when you were about six months old. A new set of teeth grows under your milk teeth and your milk teeth start to fall out when you are about six years old. These new teeth are your permanent teeth.

It is very important to look after your permanent teeth. If one of your permanent teeth comes out, you cannot grow a new one to take its place!

How to look after your teeth

- Brush them twice a day – once after breakfast, and once just before you go to bed at night.
- Don't eat sweets or foods with sugar in.
- Avoid fizzy drinks.
- Choose foods such as apples and carrots and drinks such as water and milk – all these can help to keep your teeth healthy.
- Go to the dentist for a check-up – if you have any **decay**, the dentist can give you a filling to stop it getting any worse.

Test yourself

1. Why do humans need teeth?
2. What are the three kinds of teeth called?
3. What are your milk teeth?

Remember

Incisors cut food into smaller pieces.

Canines tear up food.

Molars crush and grind up food.

You can keep your teeth and gums healthy by brushing them and by not eating sugary food.

Heart and blood

When you run around or play games you breathe faster, you get hot and you might feel tired. Sometimes you can also feel your **heart** beating faster. This means that your heart is getting oxygen to the **muscles** more quickly than usual, because they have been working hard.

Your muscles need food to keep them working. Food (**nutrients**), oxygen, water and other substances are carried around your body in the **blood**. Your heart pumps blood around your body.

Your heart is in your chest and it is protected by your ribs.

The walls of your heart are made of muscle. There are spaces inside it that are filled with blood. The heart muscle contracts (gets smaller) and squeezes blood out. This pumps blood around your body.

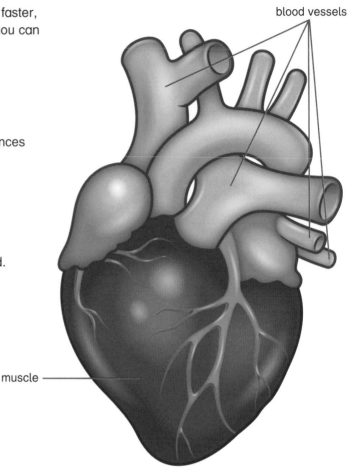

blood vessels

muscle

Arteries and veins

The blood travels around your body in **blood vessels**. These are tubes that the blood can move through. The blood vessels that carry blood from your heart to your muscles are called arteries. The ones that carry blood back to your heart are called veins. Your heart, blood and blood vessels are called your **circulatory system**.

arteries

veins

heart

What is your pulse?

You can feel the blood moving through your blood vessels in your neck or in your wrist. The movements you can feel are called your **pulse**. Each beat of your pulse is made by one beat of your heart. Your **pulse rate** is the number of beats per minute. Your pulse rate depends on what you are doing.

When you run around, your muscles need more food. This means that more blood has to flow to your muscles, so your heart has to beat faster. When you stop running around, it takes a little while for your pulse rate to go down to its normal level again.

How does exercise affect your pulse rate?

Max wanted to find out how his pulse rate changed when he exercised.

Max's pulse rate during break

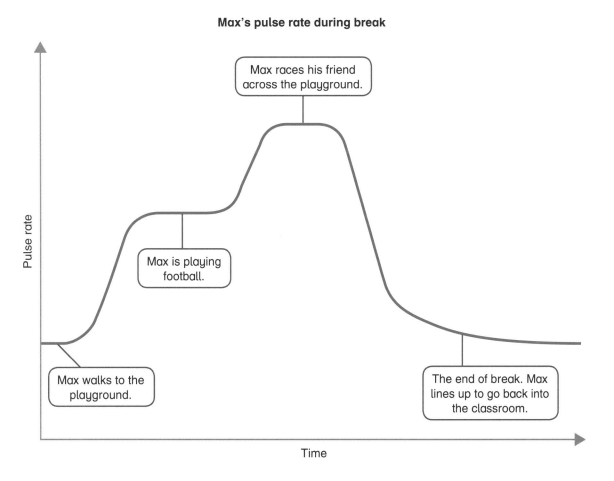

Max races his friend across the playground.

Max is playing football.

Max walks to the playground.

The end of break. Max lines up to go back into the classroom.

Pulse rate

Time

Test yourself

1. What does blood carry around your body?
2. What pumps blood around your body?
3. Which kind of blood vessel takes blood to your muscles?
4. What is your pulse rate?
5. Draw a table like this and write down all the things you do during the day. Decide if your pulse rate would be low, medium or high for each activity.

Activity	Pulse rate
Eating breakfast	Low

Remember

Food, oxygen and other substances are carried around your body in your **blood**.

Your **heart** pumps blood around your body.

Blood travels in tubes called **blood vessels**.

Arteries take blood away from your heart, and veins take it back to your heart.

Your **pulse rate** is the number of times your heart beats each minute.

The human life cycle

You were very small when you were born and your parents or carers had to do everything for you – wash you, feed you and change your nappies! Your body changes as you get older and, eventually, you might have children of your own. All these changes are part of the human **life cycle.**

Some animals can look after themselves as soon as they are born. For example, **fish** do not look after their babies. Baby fish can swim and find food as soon as they come out of their eggs.

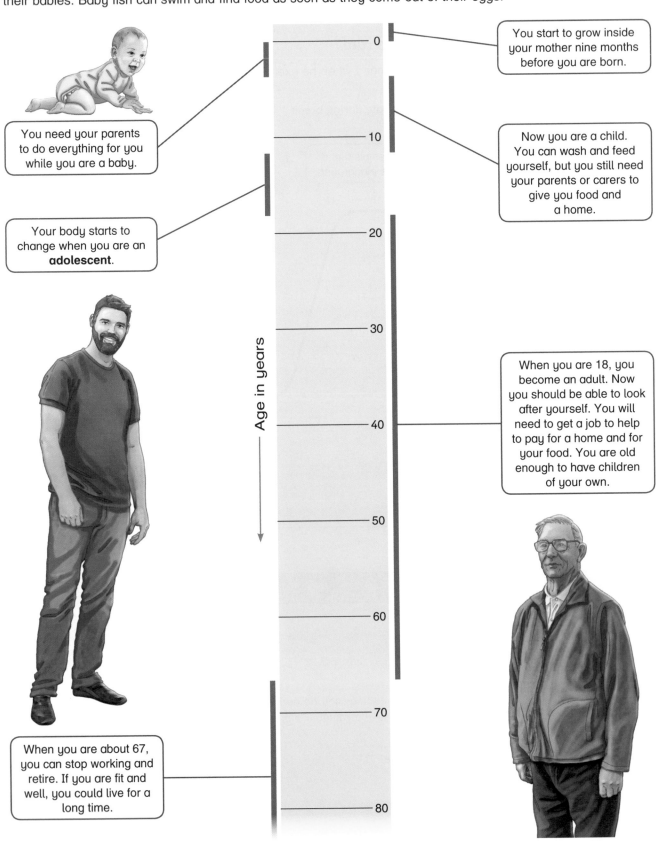

You start to grow inside your mother nine months before you are born.

You need your parents to do everything for you while you are a baby.

Now you are a child. You can wash and feed yourself, but you still need your parents or carers to give you food and a home.

Your body starts to change when you are an **adolescent**.

Age in years

When you are 18, you become an adult. Now you should be able to look after yourself. You will need to get a job to help to pay for a home and for your food. You are old enough to have children of your own.

When you are about 67, you can stop working and retire. If you are fit and well, you could live for a long time.

Puberty

Puberty is the time in your life when you are changing from a child into an adult. These changes happen while you are an adolescent.

Girls

- Breasts develop.
- Hips get wider.
- Hair starts to grow on the body.
- Bodies change inside so they are ready to start having babies.

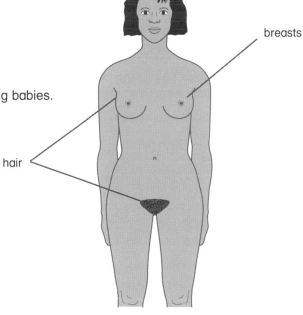

breasts

hair

Boys

- Voice gets lower.
- Hair starts to grow on the body and face.
- Penis and testicles get larger.
- Bodies change so they are ready to start making babies.

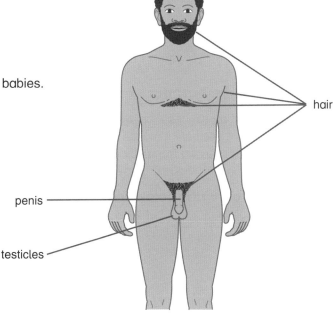

hair

penis

testicles

Old age

When you reach the age of 50 or 60 your body starts to change again. Your hair will become grey and you are more likely to need spectacles for reading.

Test yourself

1. Write down the stages in the human life cycle, in order.
2. How long did you take to grow inside your mother?
3. How old will you be when you can look after yourself completely?
4. Write down three changes that will happen to you when you go through puberty.

Remember

Your body changes as you get older. These changes are called the **life cycle**.

Puberty is the time when your body changes from being a child to being an adult.

Health

When you are healthy you feel well and you can work and play without getting too tired. You need to lead a healthy lifestyle to keep your body working well. **Diet**, exercise and **drugs** all affect your health.

- You need to eat a **balanced diet** to make sure your body gets all the substances it needs. You can read more about balanced diets on pages 20 and 21.
- You need to exercise by running around or by playing games such as football or rounders. Exercise keeps your **heart** and **muscles** strong.
- If you are ill, you can often take a drug to help you get better.

What is a drug?

A drug is a substance that can change the way your body works. If you have a cough, a headache or a sore throat, you can buy medicines. Medicines are drugs that will help you to feel better. You must always take the correct amount of a medicine: if you do not take enough, it will not work properly, but if you take too much it can harm your body.

If you have a more serious illness, such as measles or tonsillitis, you must see a doctor. The doctor will decide which medicines will make you better and how much of the medicine you need to take.

Some medicines have side effects. A side effect is something that the medicine does to you that you did not want. For example, if you take a medicine to stop you feeling sick on a car journey, the medicine can often make you sleepy. Feeling sleepy is a side effect of the medicine. People take the medicine because they think it is better to feel sleepy than to feel sick!

Drugs that can be harmful

Some drugs are not medicines. For example, alcohol is a substance that is in beer and wine. People drink alcohol because it makes them feel good. However, if they drink too much they can feel very ill the next day and too much alcohol can harm the body. If someone tries to drive a car after drinking alcohol, they may have an accident.

Tobacco contains a drug that people breathe in when they smoke cigarettes. Smoking tobacco makes some people feel good, but the substances in cigarette smoke can damage the heart and lungs.

Hygiene

You also need to keep your body clean to stay healthy. This includes washing your hands before eating and after you go to the toilet. You also need to look after your teeth – see page 25.

Test yourself

1. Write down two things you need to do to stay healthy.
2. a What are drugs?
   b What is a side effect?
   c Give an example of a side effect.
3. Write down the different ways that alcohol and tobacco can harm your body.
4. Explain how alcohol and tobacco could harm people who do not drink or smoke.

Remember

You need to exercise and eat a **balanced diet** to stay healthy.

Drugs are substances that change the way your body works.

Some drugs are medicines that can make you better if you are ill.

Alcohol and tobacco are drugs that can harm your body.

Feeding

We all need to eat food to stay alive. A plant is a **producer** because it produces food for animals to eat. A human or any other animal is a **consumer**, because it consumes (eats) the food made by plants.

Food chains

A **food chain** shows the different animals that eat each other. The arrows show the direction that the food goes through the chain. Food chains always start with a plant, because plants make their own food using light, water and air.

An animal that only eats plants is a **herbivore**. In the food chain shown below, the tadpoles are herbivores. An animal that only eats other animals is a **carnivore**. The perch and pike are carnivores. An **omnivore** eats plants and other animals.

This is a food chain for organisms in a pond.

waterweed ⟶ tadpole ⟶ perch ⟶ pike

The food chain starts with a plant: the waterweed. The waterweed feeds the tadpoles, so the waterweed is a producer.

An animal that eats plants or other animals is called a consumer, so the tadpoles, perch and pike are all consumers.

A **predator** eats other animals. The pike and perch are predators because they eat other animals.

Prey are animals that are eaten by other animals. The perch and tadpoles are prey, because other animals eat them.

An animal can be both a predator and prey. For example, the perch eats tadpoles, so it is a predator. Pike eat the perch, so the perch is also prey for a different animal.

Vegetarians

Humans are omnivores because they can eat plants and meat. However, some people choose to be herbivores: these people are known as **vegetarians**. Most vegetarians eat eggs and cheese and drink milk as well as eating foods from plants.

Test yourself

Look at this food chain to help you to answer the questions.

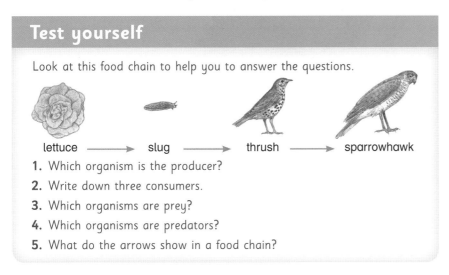

lettuce ⟶ slug ⟶ thrush ⟶ sparrowhawk

1. Which organism is the producer?
2. Write down three consumers.
3. Which organisms are prey?
4. Which organisms are predators?
5. What do the arrows show in a food chain?

Remember

We all need to eat food to live.

Plants are **producers**, and animals are **consumers**.

Predators eat **prey**.

A **food chain** shows which animals eat each other.

Food chains always start with a plant.

Evidence from fossils

Fossils are the shapes of dead plants and animals preserved in rocks. You can find out how fossils form on page 61.

Scientists can work out how old a fossil is by counting how many layers of rock there are above it. Fossils in the oldest rocks show very different kinds of living things from the ones we see around us today.

Fossils show us that living things have changed over time. Many kinds of living things no longer exist. They have become **extinct**.

This is a fossil of an animal called Archaeopteryx. These animals changed over time, and eventually became the **birds** we see around us today.

This is a reconstruction of what an Archaeopteryx looked like.

Test yourself

1. What is a fossil?
2. What does 'extinct' mean?
3. How do scientists know that living things have changed over time?

Remember

A **fossil** is the shape of a dead plant or animal preserved in rock.

Fossils show us that living things have changed over time.

Variation

Living things reproduce by producing offspring. The offspring look similar to their parents because they **inherit** features from their parents.

Offspring do not always look like their parents right away. For example, a frog lays eggs that grow into tadpoles, but then the tadpoles turn into frogs. The new frogs look very similar to the parent frogs.

Offspring usually look a little different from their parents. Your parents do not look exactly the same as each other, and you inherit some features from each parent. This means you are not exactly the same as either of your parents. Small differences between individuals of the same kind are called **variation**.

Examples of variation in humans include:

- how tall you are
- the colour of your eyes and hair
- the shape of your face, nose and mouth.

There is also variation in plants and animals. For example:

- some oak trees may grow taller than others
- some **flowers** may make bigger **seeds** than others
- some lions may be able to run faster than others.

These plants were all grown in exactly the same conditions. They are different heights because they inherited slightly different characteristics.

Test yourself

1. Write down two ways in which you may look different from a brother or sister.
2. What is the name for small differences between individuals?
3. Write down one way in which plants of the same kind may be different from one another.
4. Write down one way in which animals of the same kind may be different from one another.

Remember

Offspring **inherit** features from their parents.

Offspring look similar to their parents but they are not exactly the same.

Small differences between individuals are called **variation**.

Adaptation and evolution

Animals and plants have **adapted** to their **habitats**. This means they have special features to help them to survive there. There is more on habitats on pages 14 to 15.

Rabbits often live in a woodland habitat. They have large ears to listen for foxes and strong hind legs to help them to run away.

Earthworms live in the **soil**. They have smooth, slippery skin to help them to slide through the soil. They eat dead **leaves**.

The **fish** and plants in a pond habitat have all adapted to living underwater.

- The water lily has long stalks so that its leaves can reach the surface.
- The pond skater can walk on the surface of the water.
- The pike has large teeth to catch and eat other fish.

Sometimes the conditions in a habitat can change. This may happen because the weather conditions change or because new plants or animals move into the area. Changes to a habitat may mean that the adaptations of plants and animals are no longer as useful as they were.

Here we can see a kind of moth called a Peppered moth. The speckled pattern on its wings helps to make it harder to see when it rests on trees. This helps to protect it from **birds** that would eat it.

About 250 years ago, people in Britain started to burn more coal in factories. Smoke and soot from the coal polluted the air and covered trees. The **trunks** of trees became very dark. The Peppered moths were much easier to see on the dark trees.

Some Peppered moths are born with dark wings. These moths were not as easy to see. They were better adapted to the change in the **environment**. The dark moths were more likely to survive long enough to reproduce. Eventually most of the moths were the dark form. A change in their habitat had changed the moths.

There is not so much pollution now, so the lighter-coloured moths are now more common again.

Changes and adaptations like this can lead to very big changes in animals and plants over millions of years. This is called **evolution**.

Test yourself

1. What does 'adaptation' mean?
2. Write down two ways that rabbits are adapted to their habitat.
3. Write down one thing that could change a habitat.
4. Why do you think the light-coloured moths are more common again now?

Remember

Animals and plants have **adapted** to help them to live in their **habitats**.

Habitats can change.

Plants and animals that have adapted better are more likely to survive to reproduce.

This can lead to **evolution**.

Materials and their uses

Look around you and you will see things made of lots of different materials. Windows are made of glass. Doors and floors are made from wood and door handles are made from metal. Glass is used for windows because it is **transparent** (see-through) and wood is used for floors because it is strong.

When we describe what a material is like, we are describing its **properties**. We use different materials for different jobs, because they have different properties. The words below all describe different properties.

Words used to describe the properties of materials

There are many words that can be used to describe the properties of materials. Here are just a few.

Property	Meaning
absorbent	soaks up water easily
brittle	breaks easily if you hit it
cheap	least expensive to buy
flexible	bendy
hard	difficult to dent
light	easy to lift, not too heavy to carry
strong	difficult to break
transparent	see-through
magnetic	is attracted to a magnet

Some materials have properties that need more than one word to describe them. For example, when you are choosing a material you might need to consider:

- whether or not heat travels through the material easily (heat does not travel through wood so it is a good material to use for the handles of things that get hot – you can find out more about this on page 40).
- whether or not **electricity** travels through the material easily (electricity does not travel through plastic so this is a good material to use for the handset of a telephone, which you need to hold – you can find out more about this on page 41).
- whether or not the material looks attractive (for example, polished wood is shiny and can have attractive patterns in it).

A material is used for a particular job because of one or two of its properties. Most materials have more than one property.

Magnets attract things made from iron or steel. These are **magnetic materials**.

Plugs are made from plastic, because electricity does not go through plastic. This stops you getting an electric shock!

Towels are made from cotton because it is absorbent and flexible.

Windows are made from glass because it is transparent and hard. Glass is also brittle, which is not a useful property!

Cooking spoons are made of wood, because heat does not travel through wood easily.

Mugs and plates are made from ceramic materials, because they are hard and heat does not travel through them easily. Ceramics are also brittle, which is not a useful property.

Knives and spoons are made from steel, which is a strong and cheap metal.

Tables and cupboards are made from wood because it is hard and strong. It is also easy to make wood into different shapes and to paint or polish it so that it looks nice.

Saucepans are made of a metal called aluminium. Aluminium is light, so the pans are easy to lift.

Drinks bottles are made of plastic, because it is light and not brittle. It is also easy to make it into the right shape.

Test yourself

1. **a** Glass is used to make windows. Write down two useful properties of glass.
   b Write down one property of glass that is not useful.
2. Why are towels made from cotton?
3. Why is some furniture made of wood?
4. Why are plugs made from plastic?
5. Jumpers are often made from wool. What are the useful properties of wool?

Remember

Different materials have different **properties**, such as being strong, flexible or **transparent**.

We choose materials to make things because of their useful properties.

Testing materials

Scientists need to be able to test different materials to find out which one is best for the job. Scientists must make sure that each test they make is a **fair test**. You can find out more about fair tests on page 85.

Kitchen towels are made of paper. They are used to mop up spills. Jessica tested different kinds of paper to find out which kind is best for kitchen towels.

Jessica's experiment

Jessica tested paper from a newspaper, an exercise book and a piece of kitchen towel.

She cut all the paper into the same size squares.

  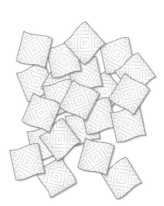

Jessica poured a small amount of water on to the table, then mopped it up using the squares of newspaper. She counted how many squares of paper she needed to mop up all the water. She did the same thing again with the exercise book paper and the kitchen towel. She used the same amount of water each time. The table shows her results.

Paper	Number of pieces needed
newspaper	2
exercise book paper	4
kitchen towel	1

Jessica found that the best paper for mopping up spills is the kitchen towel, because it did not take many pieces of paper to soak up all the water.

Jessica's test was fair because she cut all the paper into the same size squares and she used the same amount of water each time.

Test yourself

1. Write down two things that Jessica did to make her test fair.

Remember

You can test materials to find which one is best for a job.

Hot and cold

Temperature is a way of saying how hot or cold something is. You can measure the temperature of something using a **thermometer**. The units for temperature are **degrees Celsius (°C)**.

This thermometer is measuring the temperature of the air in the room. It is 21°C.

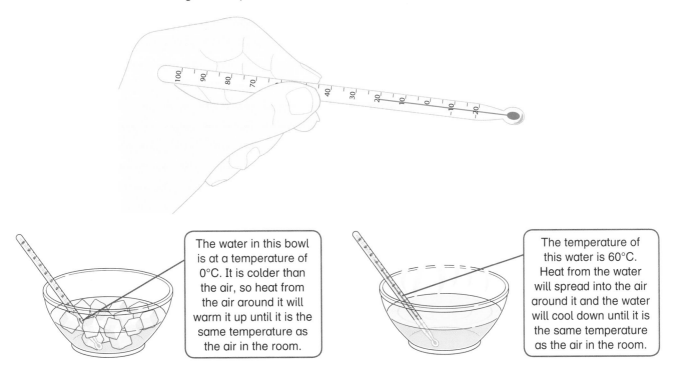

The water in this bowl is at a temperature of 0°C. It is colder than the air, so heat from the air around it will warm it up until it is the same temperature as the air in the room.

The temperature of this water is 60°C. Heat from the water will spread into the air around it and the water will cool down until it is the same temperature as the air in the room.

You can measure the temperature of water as it cools down and you can show the results in a graph.

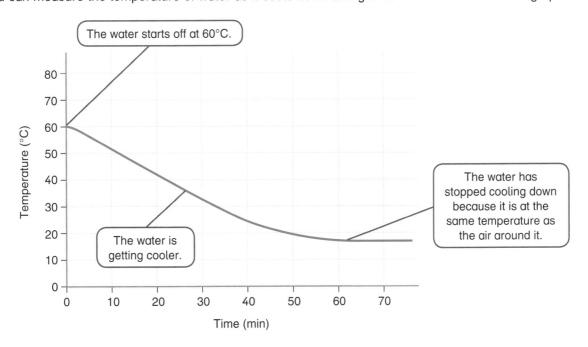

The water starts off at 60°C.

The water is getting cooler.

The water has stopped cooling down because it is at the same temperature as the air around it.

Test yourself

1. What are the units for measuring temperature?
2. What do you use to measure temperature?
3. The temperature in your bedroom is 23°C. If you leave a cup of tea in your room, what temperature will it be the next morning?

Remember

You measure **temperature** using a **thermometer**.

The units for temperature are **degrees Celsius (°C)**.

Conducting heat

Heat can travel through some materials better than others.

Thermal conductors

Heat can travel through metals very easily. This is why you can burn your fingers if you pick up a teaspoon that has been standing in hot tea for a few minutes. Metal is a good **thermal conductor**.

Thermal insulators

Heat does not travel very well through wood. Wood is a **thermal insulator**. Plastic is also a thermal insulator. Cooking spoons are usually made from wood or plastic, so that the heat from cooking food does not travel up them and burn your hand.

Keeping things warm

Thermal insulators are very useful for keeping you warm. Jumpers keep you warm because they have lots of little pockets of trapped air. Trapped air is a good thermal insulator.

This mug is made of plastic and foam, which are good thermal insulators. The hot tea inside it will stay hot for a long time, because heat cannot get out very easily.

Keeping things cool

Thermal insulators can also keep cold things cold.

This cool box is made of plastic and foam, which are good thermal insulators. It is used to keep food cold. Heat from the air outside cannot get into the box, so the food stays cold.

Test yourself

1. Write down one material that is a good thermal conductor.
2. Write down two materials that are good thermal insulators.
3. Duvets are often filled with feathers. Explain why duvets keep you warm.

Remember

Thermal conductors let heat travel through them easily.

Metals are good thermal conductors.

Thermal insulators do not let heat travel through them.

Wood and plastic are good thermal insulators.

Conducting electricity

Some materials let **electricity** flow through them. A material that lets electricity flow through it is called an **electrical conductor**. A material that does not let electricity flow through it is called an **electrical insulator**.

Is it a conductor or an insulator?

You can test a material to see if it is a conductor or an insulator using a **circuit** like this.

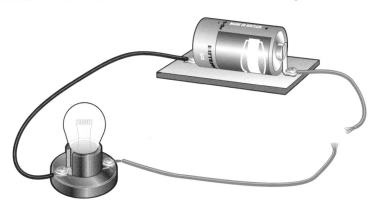

Put the material you are testing in the gap and join it to the wires on each side. If the material is an electrical conductor, electricity will flow through it and the bulb will light. You can find out more about circuits on pages 80 to 81.

Metals are good electrical conductors. Materials that are good electrical conductors are usually good thermal conductors as well.

Plastic, rubber and wood are all good electrical insulators.

Using conductors and insulators in a plug

Different parts of a plug are made from metal (an electrical conductor) and plastic (an electrical insulator), because each part of the plug has a different job.

The pins of the plug are made of metal. Metal is an electrical conductor, so electricity can flow through the pins easily.

The outside of the plug is made of plastic. Plastic is an electrical insulator, so it stops electricity flowing through you when you touch the outside of the plug.

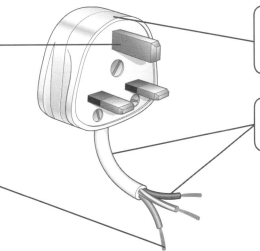

The wires are covered in plastic, to make sure you do not get an electric shock if you touch the wires.

The wires are made of metal, so that electricity can flow through them.

Remember

Electrical conductors let **electricity** flow through them easily.

Metals are good electrical conductors.

Electrical insulators do not let electricity flow through them.

Plastics are good electrical insulators.

Test yourself

1. Write down one material that is an electrical insulator.
2. Why are the pins in a plug made from metal?
3. Why are wires covered in plastic?

Solids and liquids

On pages 36 and 37, you learnt how to describe the **properties** of different materials. Another way of describing the properties of a material is to say if it is **solid** or **liquid**. Solids and liquids have different properties.

The properties of solids

Solids are usually hard and do not change shape. They are very difficult to squash and their volume (the amount of space they take up) does not change. Wood and metal are solids.

The properties of liquids

Liquids are runny. The shape of a liquid depends on the shape of the container you put it into. Liquids do not change volume, even though they can change shape. It is very difficult to squash liquids. Water and honey are liquids.

There is the same volume of water in all four containers.

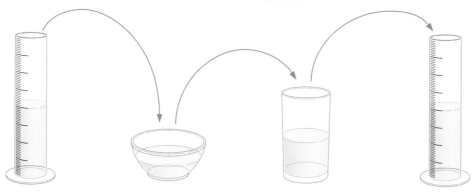

It is difficult to squash a liquid.

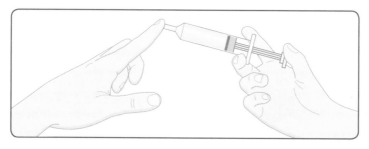

Solid or liquid?

It is difficult to decide whether some things are solids or liquids. You can pour sand like a liquid, but each separate particle of sand is a solid. You can also pour rice, flour and salt. These materials are all solids, but they behave like liquids in some ways because they are made of very tiny pieces.

Test yourself

1. Write down the names of two solid materials.
2. Write down the names of two liquid materials.
3. Write down the names of two solid materials that sometimes behave like liquids.
4. Write down three properties that all solids have.
5. Write down three properties that all liquids have.

Remember

Solids are hard and keep the same shape. **Liquids** are runny, and do not keep the same shape. They take up the shape of the container they are in.

Solids and liquids always keep the same volume.

Solids that are made of very tiny particles can behave like liquids in some ways.

Gases

Air is not a solid or a liquid. The air is made of **gases**. You cannot see air, but you know it is real because you can often feel it, especially when it is moving, such as on a windy day.

Different types of gases

There are lots of different types of gas.

- Part of the air is made of oxygen gas. All living things need oxygen to stay alive.
- The bubbles in fizzy drinks are carbon dioxide.
- Some balloons are filled with helium gas, which makes them float.
- The gas that burns in cookers is called natural gas.

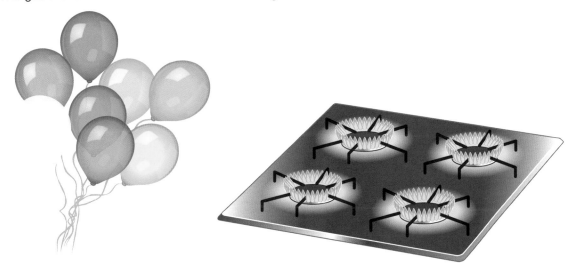

The properties of gases

Gases have different properties from solids and liquids. You can squash a gas quite easily, but you cannot squash solids and liquids.

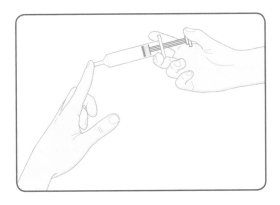 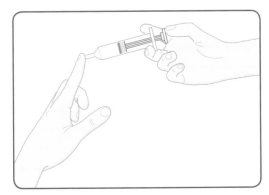

Gases spread out to fill the container they are in. You can smell perfume all over a room because the perfume evaporates into a gas and the gas spreads out.

Test yourself

1. Write down one reason we know that air is real.
2. Write down the names of four different gases.
3. Write down two ways in which gases are different from liquids.
4. Write down one way in which gases are similar to liquids.

Remember

Gases can be squashed and spread out to fill their container.

There are lots of different gases and they have different uses.

Changing state

Water can be a **solid** (ice), a **liquid** (water) or a **gas** (**water vapour** or steam). Solids, liquids and gases are the three **states** of matter.

The state of matter can change. If you let ice warm up, it will **melt** and form a liquid. If you cool the water down to 0°C it will **freeze** and turn back into ice.

Liquids can evaporate. Water in puddles dries up because the water evaporates. **Evaporation** turns water into a gas called water vapour. If you cool the water vapour down again, it will condense and turn back into liquid water. This liquid water is called **condensation**.

What happens when you boil water?

If you heat water up to 100°C it starts **boiling**. The water is evaporating so fast that bubbles of water vapour are formed in the water.

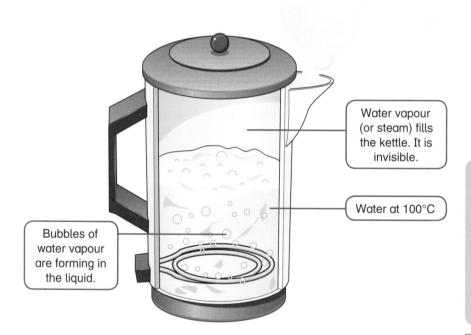

The water vapour cools down when it leaves the kettle. It condenses and forms tiny drops of water.

The 'cloud' that you can see above a kettle when it is boiling is not steam. It is tiny drops of liquid water.

Water vapour (or steam) fills the kettle. It is invisible.

Water at 100°C

Bubbles of water vapour are forming in the liquid.

A change of state is a **reversible change** because you can change a substance back to its original state by changing the **temperature**.

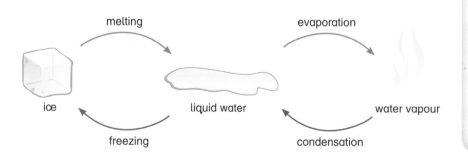

melting   evaporation

ice   liquid water   water vapour

freezing   condensation

Test yourself

1. What are the three states of matter?

2. How can you turn liquid water into ice?

3. What does 'condensation' mean?

4. What is the difference between evaporation and boiling?

Evaporation

Evaporation is what happens when a liquid turns into a gas.

When you wash clothes, they feel wet because there is a lot of liquid water in the cloth. When you hang the clothes up to dry, the water evaporates. It turns into a gas (water vapour) and mixes with the air.

Speeding up evaporation

Imagine that you have a big pile of wet washing, which you have just taken out of the washing machine. You can speed up evaporation in three ways.

1. Spread out the washing so that there is a bigger area for the water to evaporate from.

2. Dry the clothes where it is warm. Water evaporates faster when it is warm.

3. Dry the clothes in a breeze. The moving air carries the evaporated water away so that more water can evaporate into the air.

This washing will take a long time to dry.

This washing will dry quickly.

You can also dry clothes in a tumble dryer, if you have one. A tumble dryer blows warm air through the clothes. The warmth helps water to evaporate and the moving air carries the water vapour away.

> ### Remember
>
> When a **liquid** evaporates, it turns into a **gas**.
> **Evaporation** happens faster if the water is warm, if there is a large area and if the evaporated water is blown away.

> ### Test yourself
>
> 1. What does 'evaporation' mean?
> 2. Describe three ways to speed up evaporation when drying clothes and explain why they work.

Condensation

When **water vapour** cools down, it condenses and turns into a **liquid**. You can often see **condensation** happening in the bathroom.

Condensation in the bathroom

Imagine that you have just had a hot bath or shower and you are looking in the bathroom mirror. Some of the hot water has evaporated. This **evaporation** means that there is a lot of water vapour in the air. The water vapour cools down when it hits the mirror and condenses to form little drops of water. These drops of water are also called condensation. You know that they are there when you can't see your face in the mirror.

The word 'condensation' has two meanings – it means water vapour changing into liquid water and it also means the tiny drops of water that form on windows or other cold surfaces.

There is water vapour in the air all the time. If you take a can of drink out of the fridge, you will see some condensation on the outside. Water vapour in the air cools down when it touches the cold can and it condenses to form drops of water.

There is a lot of water vapour in the air that you breathe out. The air you breathe out is warm because it has been inside your body. When you breathe it out on a cold day, the water vapour cools down and condenses.

Test yourself

1. Write down two meanings for the word 'condensation'.
2. Explain why you often see condensation in the bathroom.
3. Why do you see drops of water on the outside of a can of cold drink?
4. Why can you only see your breath on a cold day?

Remember

Gases change to **liquids** in the process called **condensation**.

Condensation happens when **water vapour** cools down.

The drops of water formed by condensation are also called condensation.

Melting and boiling

Materials change **state** when they are heated up or cooled down. If you heat ice, it will **melt** when it reaches 0°C. If you cool down liquid water, it will **freeze** when it reaches 0°C. This is the freezing **temperature** of water.

Liquid water can evaporate to form a **gas**. This can happen at any temperature, but if you heat the water to 100°C, evaporation will happen as fast as it can. Bubbles of gas form inside the liquid and we say that the liquid is **boiling**. The boiling temperature of water is 100°C.

Watching what happens when ice is heated

The graph below shows what happens to the temperature of ice as it is heated up.

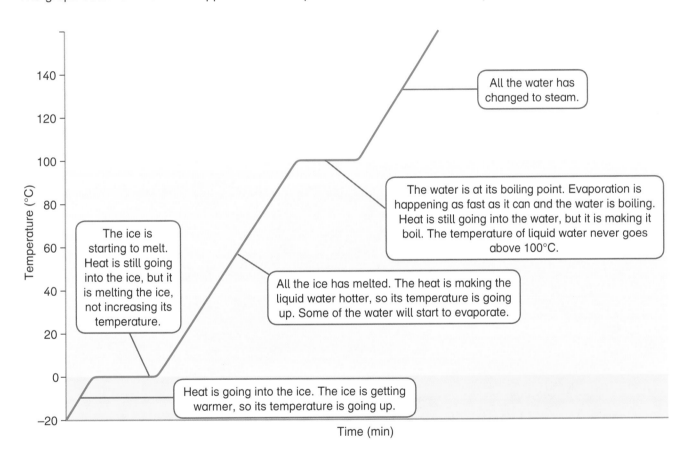

All the water has changed to steam.

The water is at its boiling point. Evaporation is happening as fast as it can and the water is boiling. Heat is still going into the water, but it is making it boil. The temperature of liquid water never goes above 100°C.

The ice is starting to melt. Heat is still going into the ice, but it is melting the ice, not increasing its temperature.

All the ice has melted. The heat is making the liquid water hotter, so its temperature is going up. Some of the water will start to evaporate.

Heat is going into the ice. The ice is getting warmer, so its temperature is going up.

Temperature (°C): 140, 120, 100, 80, 60, 40, 20, 0, −20

Time (min)

Test yourself

1. What is the boiling temperature of water?
2. What is the freezing temperature of water?
3. What is the highest temperature that liquid water can be?

Remember

Ice melts at 0°C and water boils at 100°C.

The **temperature** of **liquid** water never goes above 100°C.

The water cycle

The water that comes out of your taps was once in the sea. The **evaporation** of water from the sea, lakes and rivers forms **water vapour**. The water vapour condenses to form clouds, then the water falls as rain. Our drinking water comes from rain that is trapped in reservoirs or flows into rivers. The water has to be cleaned before we can use it. When we have used the water, it is put into drains and eventually gets back to the sea.

These changes form the **water cycle**.

Water in the clouds can fall as rain.

Water vapour in the air cools down and condenses. We see the condensed water as clouds.

Water evaporates from the sea. Evaporation happens fastest in warm places.

Water in rivers and lakes runs into the sea.

Some water evaporates from lakes and rivers.

Plants take in water from the soil. Some of this water evaporates from the plants.

Water from rivers, lakes, reservoirs or wells is cleaned before it is sent to houses.

Water from toilets, sinks and baths runs into the drains. This water is treated at sewage works to make it safe, then it is put back into rivers or the sea.

Some water soaks into the ground. We can get this water by digging wells.

f the air is very cold, he water in the clouds an freeze to form hail or snow.

Snow will melt when the Sun warms it up.

Water from rain or melted snow runs into rivers and lakes.

Some water is trapped in reservoirs.

Remember

Water evaporates from the sea and then condenses to form clouds.

Water falls from clouds as rain, then runs into rivers and lakes.

Water has to be cleaned before we use it.

Used water is treated in sewage works before it is put back into the sea.

Test yourself

1. Where can water evaporate from in the water cycle?
2. How do clouds form?
3. What happens to rain when it falls on the land?
4. What happens to water before it comes out of our taps?
5. What happens to water after we have used it?
6. Water can go through these changes of state on its way around the water cycle:
   liquid ⟶ gas ⟶ liquid ⟶ solid ⟶ liquid.
   Explain where in the water cycle each of these changes could happen.

Mixtures and filtering

Lots of different things jumbled up together are a **mixture**. For example, if you put peas and sand together, you have a mixture.

Using a sieve

You can separate a mixture using a sieve. A sieve has lots of small holes in it. Think again about the mixture of sand and peas. The sand grains are small enough to go through the holes, so they fall out of the sieve. The peas are too big to fit through the holes, so they are trapped in the sieve.

Using a filter

Some mixtures are made up of a **solid** and a **liquid**. You can mix sand with water to make a mixture. You can separate the sand and water again using a **filter**.

Filter paper has very tiny holes in it that water can go through. If you have a mixture of sand and water, the sand grains are too big to go through the holes, so they are trapped in the filter paper.

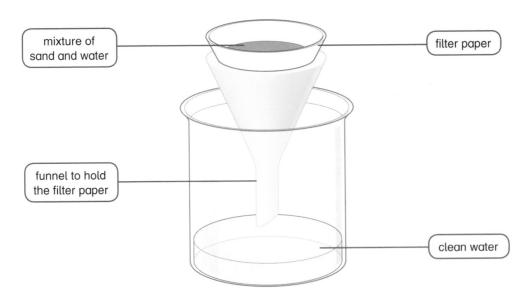

What happens when solids dissolve?

Some solids **dissolve** in water. Sugar is a solid. If you mix sugar and water, the sugar seems to disappear. You cannot see it any more, but you can tell that it is still there because the water tastes sweet. The mixture of sugar and water is called a **solution**. When a solid dissolves, it breaks up into very tiny pieces. The pieces are so small that they can go through the holes in filter paper, so you cannot separate the solid from the water by filtering.

Your cup of tea

A tea bag is a filter. When you pour **boiling** water on to a tea bag, some of the substances in the tea leaves dissolve in the water and turn it brown. The dissolved substances can go through the small holes in the tea bag. The tea leaves are too big to fit through the holes, so they are trapped in the tea bag.

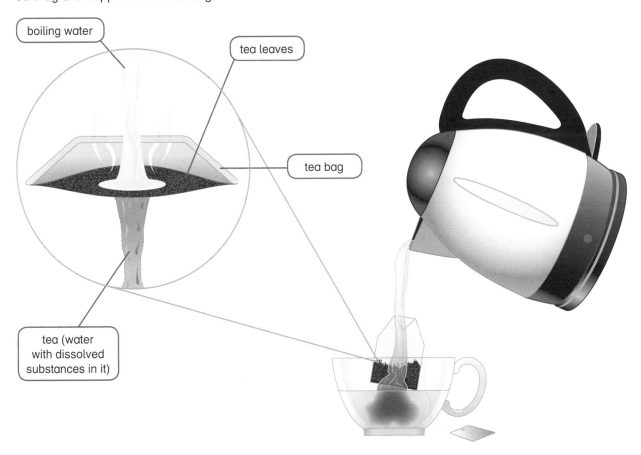

boiling water

tea leaves

tea bag

tea (water with dissolved substances in it)

Melting and dissolving

Melting and dissolving are not the same thing. A material will **melt** when it is heated. Dissolving happens when a liquid is mixed with a solid that dissolves. There are two different substances mixed together in a solution.

Remember

A **mixture** is different things jumbled together. You can use a sieve to separate things of different sizes.

You can use a **filter** to separate a **solid** from a **liquid**.

Some solids **dissolve** in water. You cannot separate them from water using a filter.

Test yourself

1. What is a sieve?
2. Why is a sieve useful for separating sand and peas?
3. How does a filter work when you use it to separate sand and water?
4. Why can't you use a filter to separate sugar and water?

More about dissolving

Have you ever tried to **dissolve** sugar lumps in cold water? It takes a long time for the sugar to dissolve. Aisha, Jack and Daisy decided to do some experiments to find out how to make sugar dissolve faster.

Aisha's experiment

Aisha wanted to find out if stirring helps sugar to dissolve. She put a spoonful of sugar into a beaker of water and measured how long it took to dissolve. Then she did the same thing again, but this time she stirred the water. She used the same amount of water and sugar each time to make sure her test was fair. Aisha used a bar chart to show her results, because she could describe the **variable** that she had changed in words – 'stirring' and 'not stirring'.

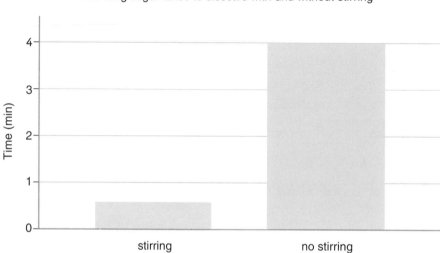

How long sugar takes to dissolve with and without stirring

Jack's experiment

Jack investigated the size of the pieces of sugar. He used caster sugar (which has very small grains), normal sugar and sugar lumps. The bar chart shows his results.

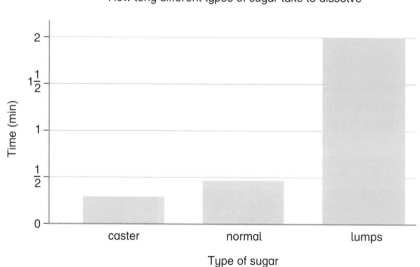

How long different types of sugar take to dissolve

Jack used a bar chart to show his results, because he could describe the sizes of the pieces in words – 'caster sugar', 'normal sugar' and 'sugar lumps'.

Daisy's experiment

Daisy wanted to find out if hot water would dissolve sugar faster than cold water. She used water at five different **temperatures** to find out the effect of temperature on the dissolving process. The graph shows her results.

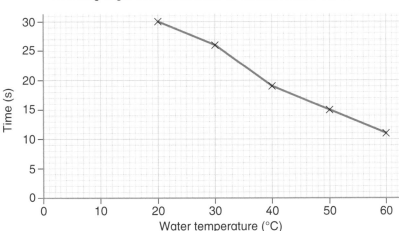

How long sugar takes to dissolve at different temperatures

Daisy used a line graph to show her results, because there are numbers between her measurements that mean something (you can find out more about graphs and charts on pages 88 and 89). For example, she could have used water at 35°C and she would have found that the sugar took 22 seconds to dissolve.

Results of the experiments

After finishing their experiments, Aisha, Jack and Daisy got together to discuss their results. They concluded that you can make sugar dissolve faster by:

- stirring the water
- using smaller pieces
- using hot water.

How much will dissolve?

Harry heard about the experiments that Aisha, Jack and Daisy had carried out and started to think some more about how a **solid** dissolves. The next morning he put six spoonfuls of sugar in his cup of hot tea. He stirred it for a minute, but he still had some pieces of sugar left at the bottom of the cup that did not dissolve. He realised that only a certain amount of a solid will dissolve in a **liquid**.

You can dissolve more of a solid if you have more liquid. For example, if you can dissolve two spoonfuls of sugar in 50cm³ of water, you can dissolve four spoonfuls in 100cm³ of water. The more water you have, the more sugar you can dissolve.

Some materials dissolve better than others. For example, you might be able to dissolve two scoops of salt in a glass of water, but you would be able to dissolve about 12 scoops of sugar in the same amount of water.

Test yourself

1. Write down three ways to make sugar dissolve faster.
2. How can you make more sugar dissolve in water?
3. What should Daisy have kept the same to make her test fair?

Remember

You can make dissolving happen faster by stirring, using hot water or using smaller pieces.

The more water you have, the more sugar you can **dissolve** in it.

Separating solutions

When a **solid** begins to **dissolve** in water, it breaks up into very tiny pieces. These pieces are small enough to go through the holes in **filter** paper. This is why you cannot use filtering to separate sugar from water or salt from water.

How to separate a solution of salty water

You can separate the different parts of a **solution** by heating it, which speeds up **evaporation**. The water in the solution evaporates and the solid is left behind. For example, if you have a pan of salty water, you can heat it until all the water has evaporated. The salt that was dissolved in the water will be left behind in the pan. If you want to get pure water from the solution, you have to trap the **water vapour** and make it condense again.

Water vapour has condensed on the lid. This water is pure water with no salt in it.

Salty water

You can also get the salt out of salty water by leaving it to evaporate, but it will take much longer for all the water to evaporate if you do not heat it.

Rain is formed when seawater evaporates and then condenses again in the air. Seawater is salty, but rainwater is not because the salt gets left behind when the water evaporates. You can find out more about the **water cycle** on pages 48 to 49.

Remember

When a **solid** dissolves, the particles are tiny, so you cannot use a **filter** to separate them.

You can separate a solid from a **solution** by letting the water evaporate, leaving the solid behind.

You can get pure water by catching the **water vapour** and condensing it.

Test yourself

1. Why can't you use filter paper to separate a mixture of salt and water?
2. How can you get salt from salty water?
3. How can you get pure water from salty water?

Reversible and irreversible changes

Reversible changes

Some materials change when you heat them. For example, if you heat ice, it will **melt** and change into **liquid** water. This is a **reversible change** because you can change the water back into ice by cooling it down until it freezes. Ice and water are both the same material, but each is in a different **state**. You can find out more about changing states on pages 44 to 47.

If you put salt into a glass of water, the salt will dissolve. You can get the salt back by letting the water evaporate. The evaporation of the water leaves the salt behind. Dissolving is a reversible change. You can find out more about dissolving on pages 51 to 54.

You can also change materials by cooling them down. If you cool water vapour, it condenses and forms liquid water. This is a reversible change, because you can easily change the liquid water back into water vapour. Most changes caused by cooling are reversible.

Irreversible changes

Some changes are not reversible so we call them **irreversible changes**. If you bake a cake, the **mixture** of flour, eggs, butter and sugar changes into cake. The cake is a new material. You cannot get the raw eggs or flour back again. Cooking food is an example of an irreversible change.

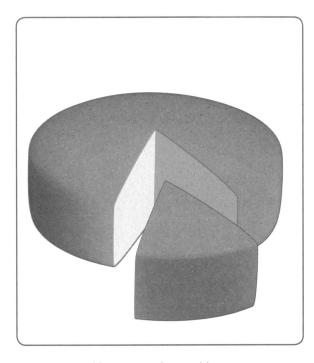

You cannot change this…

…back into this!

Remember

Changes of **state** and dissolving are **reversible changes**.

Cooking food is an **irreversible change**.

New materials are formed as a result of irreversible changes.

Test yourself

1. Write down three examples of reversible changes.
2. Is baking a cake a reversible or an irreversible change?

Irreversible changes

Irreversible changes caused by cooking

When you cook an egg, the clear, runny **liquid** changes into a white **solid**. The white solid is a new material. Cooking an egg causes an **irreversible change**. You cannot change the solid back into a runny liquid so you cannot reverse this change.

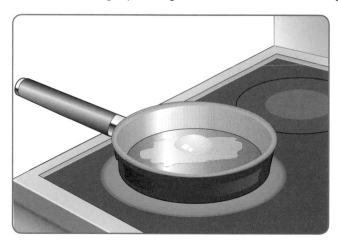 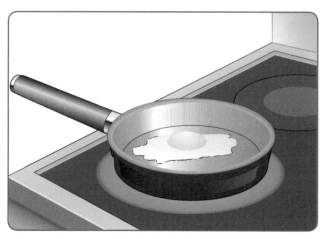

Irreversible changes caused by mixing substances

Some irreversible changes happen without heating.

Mixing concrete

Concrete is used to make buildings and paths. You can make concrete by mixing cement with gravel (small stones) and water. When the concrete dries, it goes hard. The dried concrete is a new material – you cannot get the cement, gravel and water back again. This is an irreversible change.

Iron and rust

Iron is a metal that is used for many things, including making cars. When iron is exposed to air and water it can form rust. Rust is a new substance, so rusting is an example of an irreversible change.

Bicarbonate of soda and vinegar

Bicarbonate of soda is used in baking. It can help cakes to rise. If you mix bicarbonate of soda with vinegar you will see that the **mixture** 'fizzes'. Vinegar is one of a group of substances called acids that cause irreversible changes when they are mixed with bicarbonate of soda. Part of the bicarbonate of soda has turned into a **gas**, which makes bubbles.

Irreversible changes caused by burning

Some materials burn when you heat them. **Burning** causes irreversible change.

Burning wood for warmth

You can burn wood to keep you warm. The burning logs give off heat and form an invisible gas. Ash is left after all the logs have burnt. The logs have changed into ash and invisible gases. New materials have been made, so burning is an irreversible change.

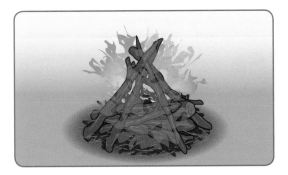

Wood burns...

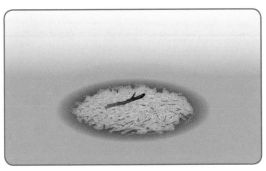

...and turns into ash.

Burning gas as a fuel

Natural gas is used to cook food or to keep homes warm. It produces invisible gases when it burns.

Take care with fire

Lots of materials in your home can burn if they are heated. Sometimes a fire starts accidentally. Fires can cause bad burns, which may even kill someone. Some materials give off poisonous gases when they burn and breathing in the smoke and gases can also kill people.

THREE RULES FOR PREVENTING FIRES

Never play with matches.

Never leave clothes or toys near heaters or fires.

Always unplug electrical things when you have finished using them.

Test yourself

1. Write down two examples of irreversible changes that happen without heating.
2. How can you tell that burning wood is an irreversible change?
3. Write down two safety rules to help prevent fires at home.
4. Describe the changes that happen to a candle when it burns and say if they are reversible or irreversible changes.

Remember

A change is irreversible if new materials are made. A change is usually irreversible if a **gas** is made. **Burning** is an **irreversible change**. A fire can harm people if they get burnt or if they breathe in poisonous gases.

Rocks

Houses and walls can be made of bricks, concrete or rock. Bricks and concrete are made from other materials, but rocks can be dug out of the ground in quarries. Small pieces of rock are called stones and small pieces that have been made smooth by the sea are called pebbles. Rocks are always underneath us, but we cannot always see them.

Some different types of rock

There are lots of different kinds of rock. Some rocks are hard and some are soft. Some rocks are **permeable**, which means that water can run through them. Rocks are made of different grains stuck together.

When you describe the size and shape of the grains in a rock, you are describing the texture of the rock.

Granite

Granite is a hard rock. It is made from different coloured grains. The grains have sharp edges, and some of them are quite big. Granite is often used for steps to buildings because it does not wear away easily.

Sandstone

Sandstone is made from lots of rounded grains stuck together. The grains are all the same size. It is sometimes used for building walls, but it is not as hard as granite and can be worn away by the weather.

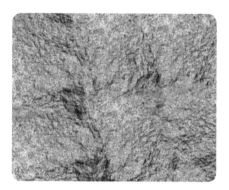

Chalk

Chalk is a soft, white rock with very small grains.
Chalk can be used for drawing because the grains
rub off very easily.

Marble

Marble is a hard rock with very tiny grains. Marble is
used for making statues because it lasts a long time
and is nice to look at.

Scientists group rocks according to their textures and their **properties**. Sandstone and
chalk are put into the same group, because they are both made from rounded grains stuck
together and they are both permeable.

Testing rocks

Sometimes you might want to find out about the properties of a rock. Two tests for rocks
are described below.

Which rock is the hardest?

You can find out which rocks are the hardest by rubbing different rocks together. The
harder rock will rub pieces off the softer rock. For example, if you rub a piece of granite
against a piece of sandstone, bits of sandstone will be rubbed off because granite is harder
than sandstone.

Is this rock permeable?

You can find out if a rock is permeable by dropping water on it. Look at the water carefully
and see if it soaks into the rock. If it soaks in quickly, the rock is permeable.

Test yourself

1. Write down two reasons you might not be able to see rocks
   underneath you.
2. Write down the names of two building materials that are not rocks.
3. Why is marble often used for statues?
4. **a** What does 'permeable' mean?
   b How can you find out if a rock is permeable?
5. Which kind of rock would be best for the wall of a building? Explain
   your answer.

Remember

Rocks are underneath us
everywhere, even though we
cannot always see them.

Rocks are made from grains
stuck together.

Rocks can be hard or soft and
some rocks are **permeable**.

Soils

Soil is made from bits of rock and from decayed bits of dead plants and animals. The decaying materials provide **nutrients** for plants growing in the soil.

Soil can have different layers in it.

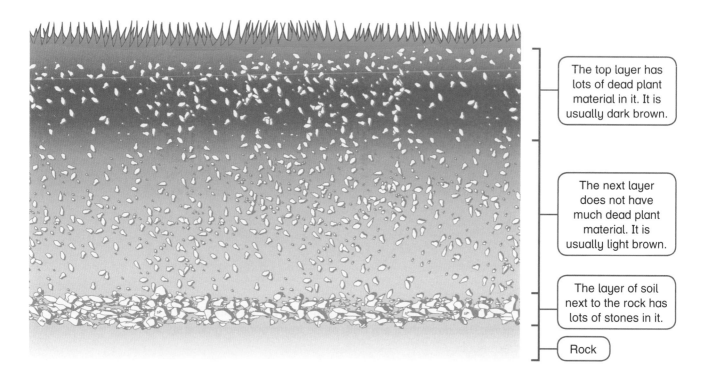

The top layer has lots of dead plant material in it. It is usually dark brown.

The next layer does not have much dead plant material. It is usually light brown.

The layer of soil next to the rock has lots of stones in it.

Rock

There are different soils in different parts of Britain, depending on the kinds of rock they are made from. Some examples are described below.

Sandy soils

Sandy soils are crumbly. Water runs quickly through sandy soils, because there are lots of air spaces.

Chalky soils

Like sandy soils, chalky soils are crumbly. Water runs quickly through chalky soil.

Clay soils

Clay soils are sticky and muddy when they are wet. Clay soils hold a lot of water, but when they dry out they go very hard and crack.

Loam soils

Loam soils have a **mixture** of sand and clay particles. They are the best soils for growing plants.

Test yourself

1. Where do the nutrients in soil come from?
2. Name one kind of soil that holds a lot of water.
3. Name one kind of soil that has a lot of air spaces in it.

Remember

Soil is made from bits of rock and decayed animals and plants.

Soil can have different layers in it.

The kind of soil depends on the kind of rock under the soil.

Fossils

Fossils are the shapes of dead plants or animals preserved in rocks. Usually just the hard parts are preserved, such as shells or **skeletons**.

Rocks get worn away by the weather and bits fall into rivers and streams. The rocks knock into each other and form smaller particles of rock. Some of these bits of rock form soils. Some form sand or mud in the sea.

When animals or plants die, they usually get eaten or rot away, but sometimes a dead plant or animal becomes buried in sand or mud before it can rot away or be eaten. Eventually more and more mud or sand builds up on top and the place with the dead animal in it turns to rock. This takes millions of years.

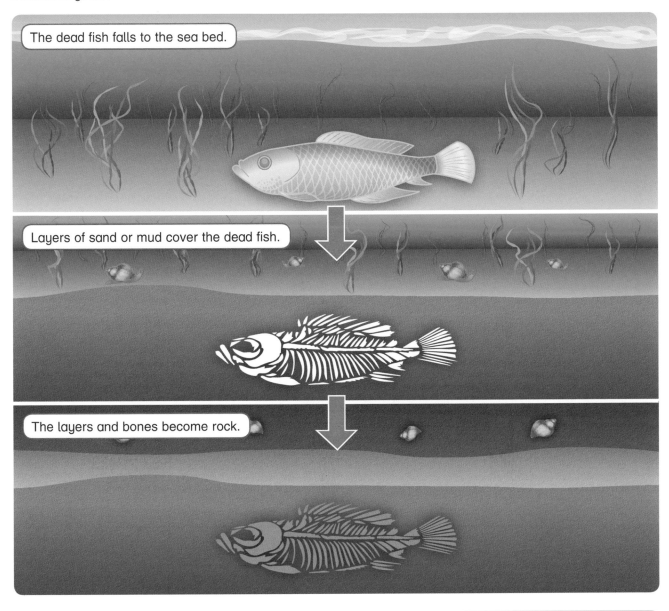

The dead fish falls to the sea bed.

Layers of sand or mud cover the dead fish.

The layers and bones become rock.

Test yourself

1. What is a fossil?
2. How long does it take for fossils to form?
3. Fossils of sea creatures with shells are more common than fossils of animals such as worms. Why do you think this is?

Remember

Dead plants or animals sometimes get covered in sand or mud before they are eaten or rot away.

The shape of the dead plant or animal becomes preserved as a **fossil**.

Light and shadows

We need light in order to see things. It is dark at **night** because no light from the Sun is reaching us.

It is important not to look directly at the Sun as it can damage your eyes.

Light can travel through some materials

Light can travel through **transparent** materials, such as glass.

Some materials are **translucent**, which means that light can go through them but you cannot see through them clearly. Bathroom windows are often made from translucent glass.

Light cannot travel through **opaque** materials such as wood or brick.

transparent

translucent

opaque

Shadows

There is a **shadow** behind the stick in the picture because light cannot go through or round the stick. Light travels in straight lines. It cannot go through opaque things, so opaque objects form shadows.

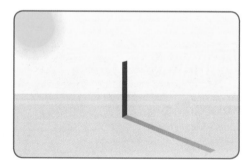

You can investigate shadows by looking at the shadow of a stick at different times during the **day**.

The shadow looks like this in the morning.

The shadow looks like this in the afternoon. The shadow has moved because, as the Earth turns on its axis, the Sun is in a different position in relation to the stick.

Experimenting with shadows

You can also experiment with shadows using a torch and two pieces of card. Use one of the pieces of card as a screen, as shown below.

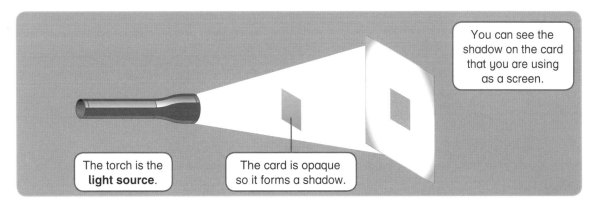

You can see the shadow on the card that you are using as a screen.

The torch is the **light source**.

The card is opaque so it forms a shadow.

If you move the screen further away from the torch, the shadow gets bigger.

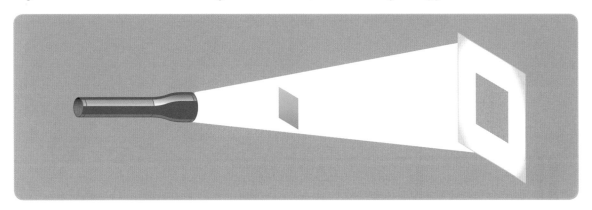

If you move the opaque card closer to the torch, the shadow gets bigger.

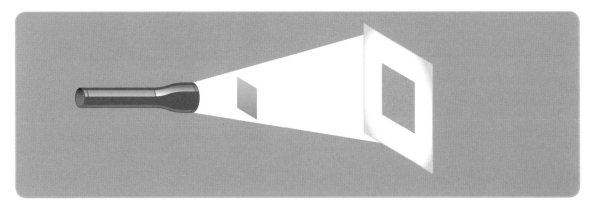

Test yourself

1. What do the words 'transparent' and 'opaque' mean?
2. Why does a stick have a shadow on a sunny day?
3. Why does the shadow of a stick change during the day?
4. What apparatus do you need to investigate shadows in the classroom or at home?
5. Describe two ways to make a shadow smaller.

Remember

Light can go through **transparent** objects but not through **opaque** ones.

Opaque objects can form **shadows**.

You can change the size of a shadow by moving the **light source** or the opaque object.

Shadows get bigger if the light source is closer to the opaque object.

Seeing and reflecting

We need light in order to see things. A **light source** is something that makes its own light. The Sun, light bulbs, candles and torches are all light sources. We see things when light from them goes into our eyes.

Most things do not make their own light. These things are not light sources. We can see them because light is reflected from them and goes into our eyes.

Light travels in straight lines

Aaliyah is looking at a candle. She puts two pieces of card between her and the candle. She can only see the candle if the holes are lined up. This is because light travels in straight lines.

Shadow shapes

Shadows have the same shapes as the **opaque** objects that block the light. This is because light travels from the light source in straight lines.

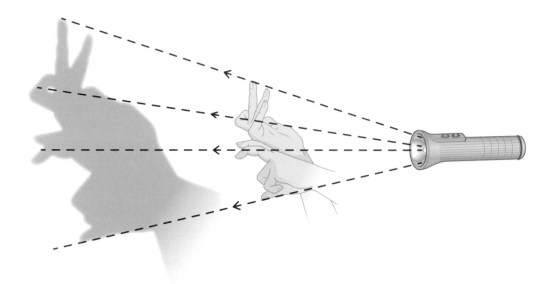

What is reflection?

Light can bounce off some materials. This is called **reflection**. Light-coloured, shiny surfaces reflect light very well. Dark, dull surfaces do not reflect light well.

We see things when light enters our eyes. We see light sources because light from them goes directly into our eyes.

We see things that are not light sources when they reflect light into our eyes.

Be safe on the roads

You can keep safe on the roads by wearing light-coloured clothes, or special reflective clothes. These clothes will reflect light much better than dark clothes and make it easier for car drivers to see you.

Test yourself

1. Why are shadows the same shape as the objects that cause them?
2. Why should you wear light-coloured clothes if you go out at night?
3. Draw a diagram to show how light travels from a light bulb to your eyes.
4. Draw a diagram to show how light travels to let you see a car on a sunny day.

Remember

Light travels in straight lines.

We see things when light goes into our eyes. **Reflection** happens when light bounces off things. Light-coloured, shiny materials are best at reflecting light. Light changes direction when it is reflected.

Sound and vibrations

Making different sounds

Sounds are made when things **vibrate** (move backwards and forwards quickly). If you make a noise using a ruler, you can see that the ruler is vibrating.

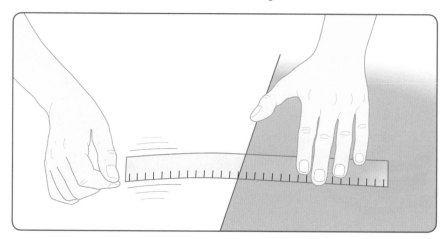

When you play a guitar, you pluck the strings and make them vibrate. The vibrating strings make the sound.

The skin of a drum vibrates when you hit it, and makes a sound.

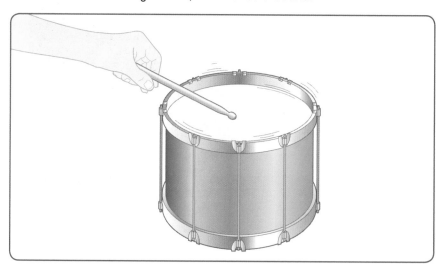

When you blow into a recorder, the air inside the recorder vibrates. It is this vibrating air that makes a sound.

Making sounds using your voice

You cannot see anything vibrating when you talk, but if you put your fingers on your throat you can feel that something is vibrating inside you!

You can make lots of different sounds using your voice. The sounds that you make can be loud or quiet. You can also make high or low sounds. A high sound has a high **pitch** and a low sound has a low pitch. You will learn more about loudness and pitch on pages 68 and 69.

How you hear sounds

You hear sounds when the vibrations travel to your ears. When your friends call out to you, the vibrations from their mouths travel through the air to your ears. Air is a **gas**. Sound can travel through gases.

If you put your ears under the water in the bath or at the swimming pool, you can still hear sounds. Water is a **liquid** and sound can travel through liquids.

Sounds can also travel through a **solid**. If you are in a room with the doors and windows shut, you can still hear things that are happening outside. Sounds can travel through glass, bricks and wood.

Is there sound in space?

Sound cannot travel if there is nothing for it to travel through. Astronauts in space cannot talk directly to each other because there is no air for sound to travel through. Instead, they have to use radios to speak to one another.

Noise

Sometimes sounds are too loud. Some sounds, such as lorries on the road outside, are annoying. Some sounds are so loud that they can damage our ears. Annoying sounds are sometimes called noise.

The loudness of a sound depends on how far away the source of the sound is. Sounds from nearby sources are much louder than sounds from distant sources.

Too noisy!

You can cut down the amount of sound in a house by using soft materials such as curtains and carpets. These materials absorb some of the vibrations and make the sounds quieter.

Sometimes you cannot stop things making sounds, so you have to protect your ears instead. Special ear muffs can stop loud noise damaging your ears.

Test yourself

1. **a** What vibrates when you play a guitar?
   b What vibrates when you play a drum?
2. What does 'pitch' mean?
3. Which materials can sound travel through?
4. How can you make a house quieter?
5. Why do some people need to wear ear muffs at work?
6. Why do pilots of aeroplanes need to use radios to talk to controllers on the ground?

Remember

Sound is made by vibrations.

Sounds can be loud or quiet.

Sounds can have a high or low **pitch**. Sounds can travel through **solids**, **liquids** and **gases**.

Sounds cannot travel in space because there is nothing for the vibrations to travel through.

Sounds can be absorbed by soft materials. Loud sounds can damage your ears.

Pitch and loudness

High and low

Musical instruments can make sounds with different **pitches**.

On a xylophone, the long bars make notes with a low pitch and the short bars make notes with a high pitch.

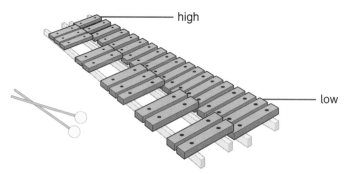
high
low

Small drums make higher-pitched sounds than big drums. You can also make the pitch of a drum higher by tightening the skin.

Changing pitch when playing a guitar

When you play a guitar, you can change the length of the strings by putting your fingers on them. When you pluck a string it will **vibrate**.

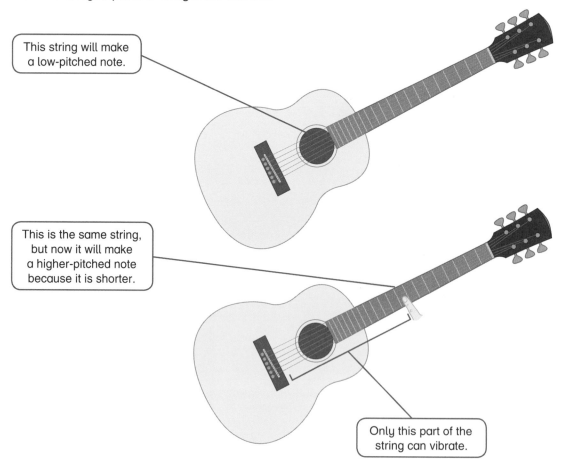

This string will make a low-pitched note.

This is the same string, but now it will make a higher-pitched note because it is shorter.

Only this part of the string can vibrate.

You can make a higher note on a guitar by:

- making the string shorter by putting your finger on it
- making the string tighter
- using a thinner string.

Changing pitch when playing a wind instrument

Some instruments make sounds because the air inside them is vibrating. These instruments are called wind instruments. The length of the air inside the instrument is called the air column. Long air columns make lower sounds than short ones. The longer the air column, the lower the pitch.

You can change the length of the air column in a trombone by moving the slide in and out.

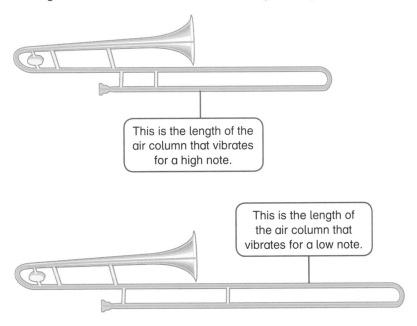

This is the length of the air column that vibrates for a high note.

This is the length of the air column that vibrates for a low note.

Loud and soft

Musical instruments can make loud sounds or soft, quiet sounds. You can make loud sounds on drums by hitting them hard and quiet sounds by hitting them gently. When you blow into a recorder, you make loud sounds by blowing hard and quiet sounds by blowing gently.

Remember

Longer or bigger instruments make lower-pitched sounds than shorter or smaller ones.

You can increase the **pitch** of a drum by tightening the skin.

You can increase the pitch of a guitar by tightening the string, making it shorter or using a thinner string.

You can increase the pitch of a wind instrument by making the air column shorter.

Test yourself

1. How do you make a loud sound on a recorder?
2. How can you make a quiet sound on a drum?
3. How can you make a low-pitched sound on a trombone?
4. Write down three ways to make a low note on a guitar.

Earth, Sun and Moon

Earth

The Earth is the planet we live on. It is shaped like a **sphere**.

How do we know that the Earth is a sphere?

We know that the Earth is a sphere because astronauts have taken photographs of the Earth from space.

However, people knew that the Earth was a sphere even before astronauts went into space. Some of the evidence for this idea was:

- when ships sailed away, the bottom part of the ship disappeared first
- the **shadow** of the same object was a different length in different places
- ships had sailed all the way around the world without falling off the edge!

The Earth does not look like a sphere when we stand on it, because it is so big. You have to be a long way from the Earth before you can see that it is spherical.

The diameter of the Earth is nearly 13 000km.

Sun and Moon

The Sun and the Moon are also spheres. The Moon is smaller than the Earth. The Sun is much bigger than the Moon and the Earth, but it is also much further away, which is why the Sun and the Moon look about the same size.

If you drew the Sun to the same scale as used in the diagram above, it would be over 50 centimetres across and nearly 6 metres away.

Test yourself

1. **a** What shape is the Earth?
   b Describe one piece of evidence for this idea.
2. Which is the biggest: the Earth, the Moon or the Sun?
3. Which is closest to Earth: the Sun or the Moon?

Remember

The Earth, Sun and Moon are **spheres**. The Earth is bigger than the Moon. The Sun is much bigger than the Earth, but it is a long way away.

Day and night

The Sun seems to move across the sky each **day**, but it is not really moving across the sky. The Earth is spinning, so the Sun seems to move because we are standing on a spinning Earth.

You must never look at the Sun directly because it could damage your eyes, but you can see how the Sun seems to move by looking at the shadow of a stick.

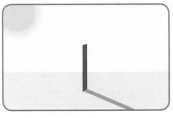
Morning – the Sun rises in the east.

Midday – the Sun is above us.

Evening – the Sun sets in the west.

Our spinning planet

The diagrams below show why the Sun seems to be moving across the sky.

The Sun seems to be in the east.

The Earth has spun round a little, so now the Sun seems to be above you.

The Earth spins a bit more and now the Sun seems to be in the west.

How long does it take the Earth to spin around?

The Earth spins round once every 24 hours.

It is daytime in the parts of the Earth facing towards the Sun.

It is night-time in the parts of the Earth facing away from the Sun.

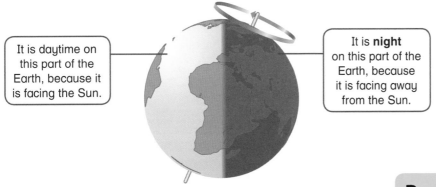

It is daytime on this part of the Earth, because it is facing the Sun.

It is **night** on this part of the Earth, because it is facing away from the Sun.

Test yourself

1. Does the Sun rise in the east or the west?
2. Why does the Sun seem to move across the sky?
3. How long does it take for the Earth to spin around once?
4. Describe how the shadow of a stick changes during the day.

Remember

The Sun rises in the east and sets in the west.

The Sun seems to move because the Earth is spinning.

It is daytime when our part of the Earth is facing the Sun.

The solar system

The Earth's orbit

The Earth spins round, which is why we have **day** and **night** – this is explained on page 71. The Earth is also moving around the Sun. It takes one **year** for the Earth to go around the Sun once. There are 365 days in a year. The path that the Earth takes around the Sun is its **orbit**.

The Earth really takes $365\frac{1}{4}$ days to orbit the Sun once. We can't have a quarter of a day, so every four years we have a leap year, which has 366 days in it.

The Moon's orbit

The Moon orbits the Earth. This means that the Moon moves around the Earth. It takes the Moon 28 days to go around the Earth once.

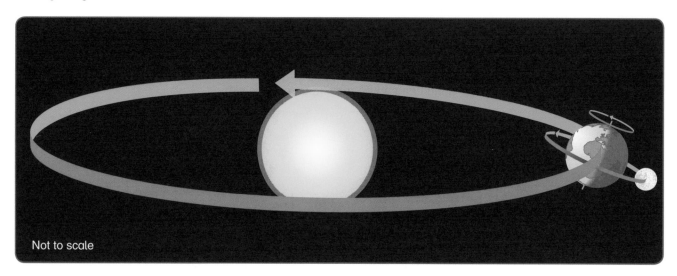

Not to scale

Seeing the Moon

The Sun is a star, just like all the other stars in the sky. It looks much bigger than the other stars because it is much closer to the Earth. The Sun is a **light source**.

We see the Moon because it reflects light from the Sun.

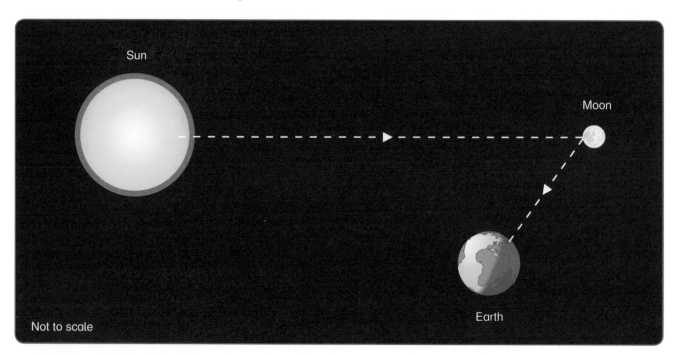

Not to scale

The solar system

The Earth is a planet. It does not make its own light. The Earth is just one of eight planets orbiting around the Sun. Some of these planets have moons of their own. The **solar system** is made up of the Sun and all the objects moving around it.

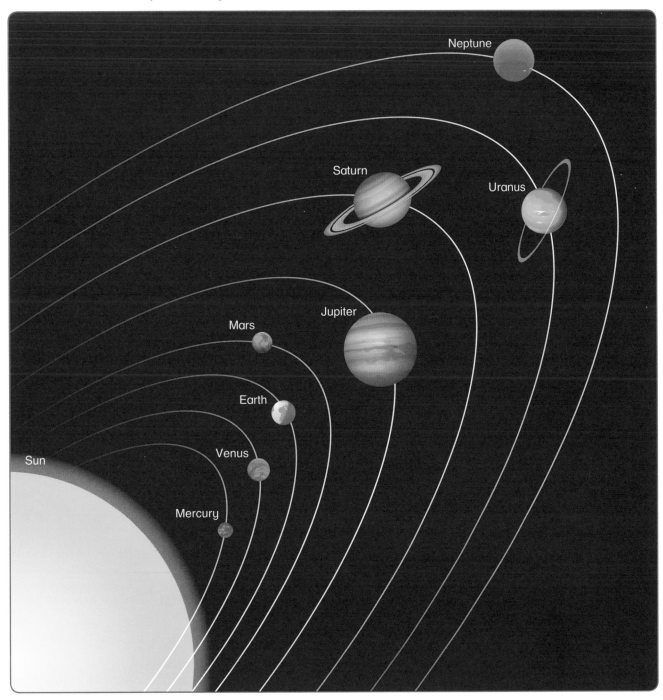

Test yourself

1. How long does it take the Earth to go around the Sun once?
2. How long does it take the Moon to go around the Earth once?
3. How can we see the Moon?
4. How many planets are there in the solar system?
5. Write down one difference between a star and a planet.

Remember

The Earth moves around the Sun. It takes 365¼ **days**, or one **year**, to go around the Sun once.

The Moon goes around the Earth once every 28 days.

There are eight planets in the **solar system**. The planets move in **orbits** around the Sun. The Sun is a star.

Forces and movement

Pushes and pulls are both **forces**. Forces can change the shape of things. They can also make things begin to move or make moving things speed up or slow down.

Many forces need two things to be touching, such as when you lift a bag or close a door. Some forces, such as magnetism and **gravity**, do not need things to be touching. You will learn more about these forces on pages 76 and 77.

Measuring forces

We can measure forces using a **forcemeter**. A forcemeter has a spring inside it. If you pull it gently, the spring only stretches a little way. If you use a bigger force (pull harder), the spring stretches further. The units for measuring forces are **newtons (N)**.

Friction

Friction is a force that slows down moving objects. Look at the picture below. There is friction between the boxes and the table. You can measure the amount of friction using a forcemeter.

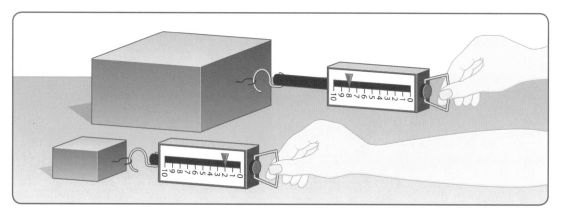

It is easiest to pull the blocks on a smooth surface. Smooth surfaces have the least friction, rough surfaces have the most friction.

Is friction useful?

Friction can be useful. For example, friction between the road and tyres stops cars and bicycles skidding on the road. Roads have rough surfaces to increase the friction.

Sometimes you do not want much friction, such as on a playground slide. Slides have very smooth surfaces so that friction is low and you can go fast!

Slowing down

Objects are slowed down when they move through water and air. Water **resistance** and air resistance are both kinds of friction.

Water resistance

Water resistance slows down things that are moving through water, such as boats and fish. Fish have a special smooth shape to reduce water resistance and let them swim fast.

Air resistance

Air resistance slows down things that are moving through the air. For example, parachutes have a large air resistance so they fall slowly. Birds have a smooth shape so they have a low air resistance and can fly fast.

Test yourself

1. What is inside a forcemeter?
2. What are the units for measuring force?
3. What is friction?
4. How can you reduce the friction between two solid objects?
5. How can you reduce the amount of water resistance on something?
6. The wind can push on things. Explain why the force from the wind would be greater on a tree than it would be on a lamp post.

Remember

Forces are pushes or pulls. They can change the shape or speed of things. The units for forces are **newtons (N)**.

Friction is a force that slows down moving objects. Friction is least when the surfaces are smooth.

Water **resistance** and air resistance are kinds of friction.

Water resistance and air resistance are small when things have smooth shapes.

Effects of forces

Gravity

Gravity is a **force** that pulls everything downwards towards the Earth. The **weight** of something is the force of the Earth's gravity pulling on it. Weight is a force, so it is measured in **newtons (N)**.

If an object is not resting on anything, it will fall downwards because of the force of gravity between the Earth and the object.

Pulleys, levers and gears

We can use some simple mechanisms to make moving things easier.

Pulleys

The weight of this box makes it difficult to lift. The man cannot pull hard enough to lift it.

A **pulley** is a rope that runs over a set of little wheels. Pulleys can allow a small force to have a great effect.

Levers

A **lever** is a long pole that can be used to give a small force a greater effect. Longer levers magnify the force more than short ones.

very big force needed to move rock

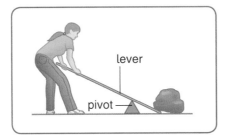

smaller force needed

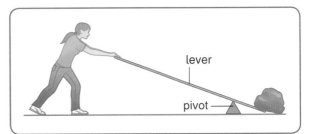

much smaller force needed

Gears

Gears are wheels with teeth on the outside. Combinations of gear wheels can be connected with chains or they can touch directly.

When you ride a bicycle, the pedals make a gear wheel go around. This is connected to the back wheel by a chain. On most bicycles, the chain can be moved from one gear wheel to a bigger or smaller one.

The chain is on the smallest gear wheel attached to the back wheel of the bicycle. It is quite hard to pedal the bike, but you can go very fast.

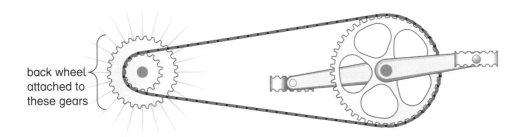

back wheel attached to these gears

The chain is on the largest gear wheel attached to the back wheel of the bicycle. The force you put on the pedals has a bigger effect. This gear is good for cycling up hills.

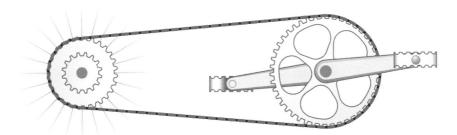

Test yourself

1. What is gravity?
2. What is weight?
3. Write down three mechanisms that can allow a small force to have a greater effect.
4. Explain how gears help you to ride a bike.

Remember

Gravity is a **force** that pulls things downwards towards the Earth.

The force of gravity on you is your **weight**.

Pulleys, **levers** and **gears** can give a small force a greater effect.

Magnets and magnetic materials

Magnetic materials

A **magnet** can attract things made of iron because iron is a **magnetic material**. The **force** from a magnet lets you pick up things such as paper clips or food cans that have iron in them.

Iron is a magnetic material because it can be picked up by a magnet. Steel is a metal that is mainly made from iron, so it is also a magnetic material.

Not all metals are magnetic materials. For example, drinks cans are made from a kind of metal called aluminium, which is not a magnetic material. So you cannot pick up aluminium cans using a magnet. This is useful for recycling because you can easily separate steel and aluminium cans using a magnet.

Attracting and repelling

The two ends of a magnet are called the **north pole** and the **south pole**. Two magnets attract each other if a north pole of one magnet is put next to the south pole of another magnet. If you put two north poles close to each other or two south poles, you can feel the magnets **repel** (push away). We can use arrows to show the directions of the forces.

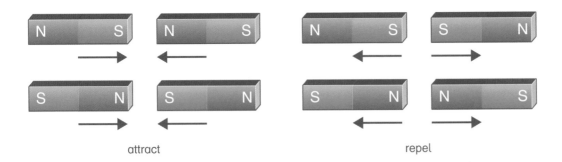

attract   repel

Using electricity

Electricity is very useful. We use it to light up our homes and make things such as TVs, computers and washing machines work.

Using mains electricity

Useful machines that use electricity are called appliances and they need a lot of electricity. They have to be plugged into sockets in the wall, which provide **mains electricity**. The electricity that comes through the mains is powerful enough to kill you if you touch it.

Using cells

Smaller things, such as torches, radio-controlled cars and mobile phones, do not need so much electricity to work. They use electricity from **cells**. A cell is much safer to use than mains electricity because the electricity it provides is not powerful enough to harm you.

Be safe!

You can use mains electricity safely if you follow the simple rules shown below.

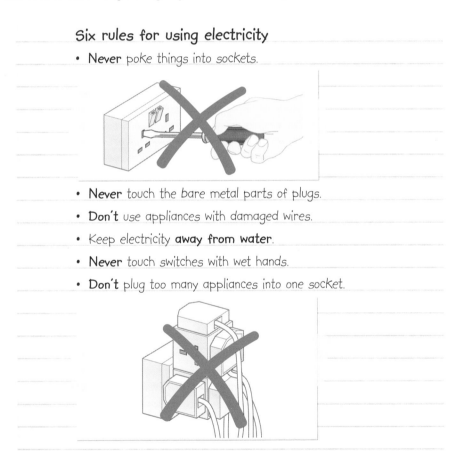

Six rules for using electricity

- **Never** poke things into sockets.
- **Never** touch the bare metal parts of plugs.
- **Don't** use appliances with damaged wires.
- Keep electricity **away from water**.
- **Never** touch switches with wet hands.
- **Don't** plug too many appliances into one socket.

Test yourself

1. **a** Write down the names of two appliances that use mains electricity.
   b Why do these appliances need to use mains electricity?
2. List three things that use cells.
3. Why are cells safer than mains electricity?
4. Write down five rules for using electricity safely.

Remember

Mains electricity can kill you.

Cells are safe to use because they do not provide very much **electricity**.

Keep safe by following the safety rules for using electricity.

Electrical circuits

This light bulb will light up because there is a **cell** and wires joining the cell to the bulb. One wire has to be joined to each side of the bulb. This is called a **circuit**.

Why doesn't the bulb light up?

This bulb will not light up because there is a gap in the circuit.

This bulb will not light up because both wires are fixed to one side of the bulb.

Using a switch

This is a switch. It makes it easy to turn the bulb on or off.

The bulb is off here because there is a gap in the circuit.

If you push the switch down, it closes the gap in the circuit. The bulb lights up.

Parts of a circuit

There is a complete circuit inside everything that uses **electricity**. A circuit is made up of several different **components**, for example:

- a source of electricity, such as a cell
- a switch
- metal wires, covered in plastic
- a light bulb, if light is required.

Electricity will only flow if there is a complete looped pathway for it to flow around.

A simple circuit

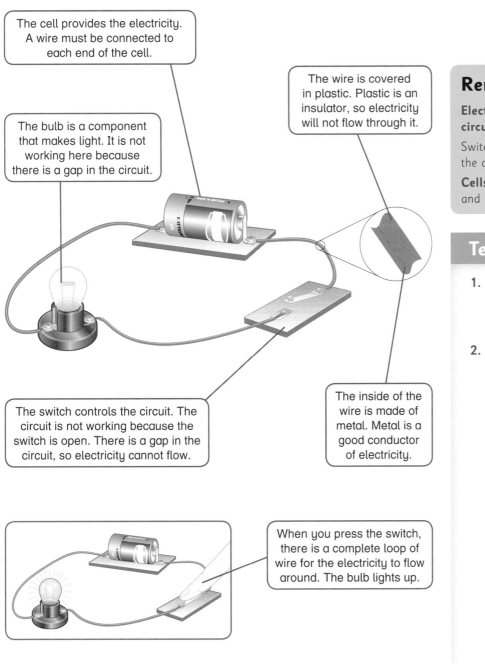

The cell provides the electricity. A wire must be connected to each end of the cell.

The wire is covered in plastic. Plastic is an insulator, so electricity will not flow through it.

The bulb is a component that makes light. It is not working here because there is a gap in the circuit.

The switch controls the circuit. The circuit is not working because the switch is open. There is a gap in the circuit, so electricity cannot flow.

The inside of the wire is made of metal. Metal is a good conductor of electricity.

When you press the switch, there is a complete loop of wire for the electricity to flow around. The bulb lights up.

Other circuit components include:

- buzzers, which make a noise
- motors, which spin around.

Test yourself

1. **a** Why are the insides of wires made of metal?
   b Why are the outsides of wires made of plastic?

2. Why won't the bulbs work in these circuits?

   a

   b

   c

   d

Changing components

Components are parts of an electrical **circuit**. **Cells**, bulbs, motors, switches and buzzers are all components.

A cell provides the **electricity** in a circuit. The voltage written on the side of a cell tells you how much electricity it provides. A 4.5V cell provides more electricity than a 1.5V cell. You can make more electricity flow in a circuit by using more than one cell.

Adding more cells

The bulb shown here will light up with a 1.5V cell.

The bulb will be brighter with two 1.5V cells. If you have a buzzer in the circuit instead of a bulb, it will be louder with two cells than with one.

If there is too much electricity flowing around the circuit, the bulb may break. You have to make sure you use the right kind of bulb for the amount of electricity in the circuit.

Adding more bulbs

You can change the brightness of bulbs by putting more bulbs in the circuit.

This bulb is bright.

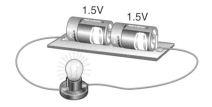

If you put another bulb in, the electricity is shared between the bulbs so they are not as bright.

The above examples show that you can make bulbs brighter by:
- using more cells
- using fewer bulbs.

Test yourself

1. How can you tell how much electricity a cell will provide?
2. How can you make the bulbs in a circuit dimmer?
3. What might happen if you put too many cells into a circuit?
4. Explain two ways in which you can make the bulbs in this circuit brighter.

Thin wires

You can change the brightness of bulbs in a circuit by changing the number of bulbs. If you put more bulbs into the circuit, the bulbs will be dimmer. This is because it is more difficult for the electricity to flow through them all, so less electricity flows through the circuit. Bulbs are dimmer when there is less electricity flowing. You can also make bulbs dimmer by putting a piece of thin wire into the circuit. This is shown by the experiment described below.

Poppy's experiment

Poppy did an experiment to find out if the length and the thickness of the wire made a difference to the brightness of the bulbs.

1. First she tried a long wire.

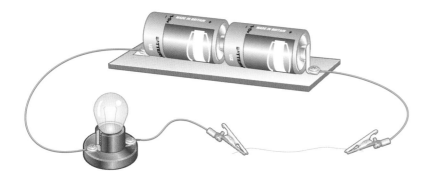

2. Then she used a shorter piece of the same wire. She used the same cells and bulb to make sure her test was a **fair test**. She found that the bulb was brightest when the wire was short.

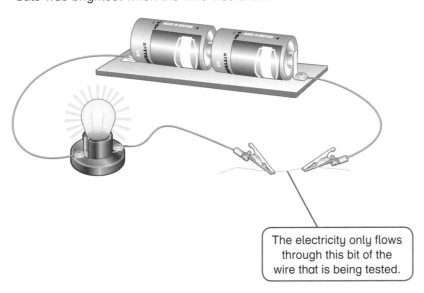

The electricity only flows through this bit of the wire that is being tested.

3. Then Poppy used a thick piece of wire, and then she used a thin piece of wire. The bulb was brightest when she used the thick wire.

Poppy found that:

- the shorter the wire, the brighter the bulbs
- the thicker the wire, the brighter the bulbs.

Poppy's experiment shows that it is easier for electricity to flow through short, thick wires than long, thin ones. More electricity will flow around the circuit, so the bulbs will be brighter.

Remember

Adding bulbs or wires makes it more difficult for **electricity** to flow in a **circuit**.

If it is difficult for electricity to flow, less of it will flow round the circuit and bulbs will be dimmer.

It is harder for electricity to flow through long, thin wires than through short, thick wires.

Test yourself

1. What happens to the brightness of a bulb if you add another bulb to the circuit?

2. Is it easier for electricity to flow through a thin wire or a thick wire?

3. If you put a long piece of wire into a circuit, will the bulbs get brighter or dimmer?

4. What did Poppy have to keep the same in her second experiment (step 3) to make sure her test was fair?

Drawing circuits

We can use symbols to draw an electrical **circuit**. A symbol is a shape that represents something else. It is easier to draw a circuit using symbols than it is to draw pictures of the **components**.

It is easier to draw this...   ...than this.

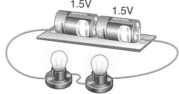

So that everyone can understand circuit diagrams, we always use the same symbol for each component. The symbols you need to know are shown in the table below.

Circuit diagrams – the eight symbols you need to know		
Name	**Picture**	**Symbol**
cell		+ −
wire		
battery		
open switch		
closed switch		
bulb		
motor		M
buzzer		

Cells and batteries

The proper scientific name for this is a **cell**.

A **battery** is two or more cells used together.

Remember

We use symbols to draw **circuits**. You need to learn all the symbols on this page.

Test yourself

1. Draw the symbols for a bulb, a cell and a motor.

2. What does this symbol represent?

3. Use symbols to draw a circuit diagram of this circuit.

Fair tests

When you are doing a scientific experiment, you must make sure that your test is a **fair test**. This means that you must only change one **variable** at a time.

Nylah's experiment

Nylah did an experiment to find out how much **friction** there was on different surfaces. She did two tests.

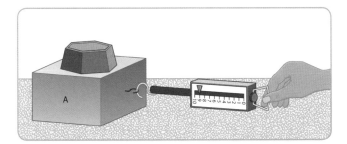 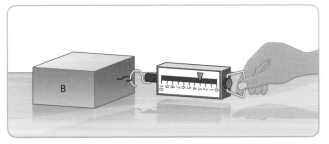

It was hardest to pull block A. This was not a very good experiment, because Nylah cannot tell whether the friction was increased by the rough surface, the size of the box or the **weight** on the box.

Nylah's test was not a fair test because she changed several factors at the same time.

Jacob's experiment

Jacob also wanted to find out about friction. First, he made a list of all the variables that could affect the amount of friction. This is Jacob's list.

> These things could affect the amount of friction:
> * the size of the box
> * the weight on the box
> * the roughness of the surface.

Jacob decided to test the roughness of the surface. He kept the other factors the same.

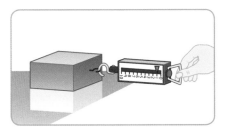 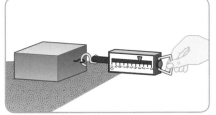 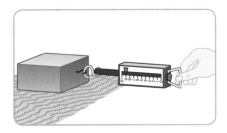

Jacob's test was a fair test because he only changed one variable.

Test yourself

1. What is a variable?
2. How many variables can you change if you are doing a fair test?
3. Imagine you are investigating what a plant needs to grow well. Write down all the factors that could affect the plant.

Remember

Variables are the things that could affect your experiment.

In a **fair test**, you can only change one variable at a time.

Measuring and units

In most scientific **investigations** you need to measure things. Sometimes you just need to count things (such as the number of woodlice under a stone), but you usually need to use equipment to measure things.

When you measure something, it is very important to include the units. Saying that a worm is 7 long does not really mean anything – you could mean 7 millimetres or 7 metres!

The table shows some of the measuring instruments you might use in scientific investigations and the units to use.

Measurement	Instrument		Units	
length	ruler or tape measure		metres centimetres millimetres	m cm mm
temperature	thermometer		degrees Celsius	°C
force	forcemeter		newtons	N
time	stopwatch		minutes seconds	min s
capacity (volume)	measuring cylinder		centimetres cubed*	cm^3

* $1cm^3$ is the same capacity as 1ml – some measuring cylinders are marked in cm^3 and some in ml, but they both mean the same.

Measuring temperature

When you are measuring **temperature**, remember that a **thermometer** reads the temperature of whatever it is standing in.

> **Remember**
>
> When you write down a measurement, always include the units.

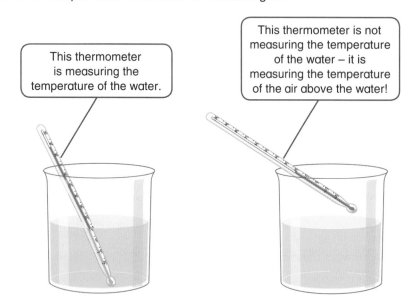

This thermometer is measuring the temperature of the water.

This thermometer is not measuring the temperature of the water – it is measuring the temperature of the air above the water!

Test yourself

1. **a** What would you use to measure the thickness of a book?
   b What units would you use?

2. **a** What would you use to measure the amount of water in a glass?
   b What units would you use?

Tables

A table is a way of presenting information that is easy to understand. You need to draw a table ready for your results before you start an experiment, so that you have somewhere to write down your measurements.

Samir's experiment

Samir did an experiment to find out how far an elastic band stretched when he hung different **weights** on it. This is the table he drew for his results.

This is what Samir was changing, so it goes in the first column.

These are the weights that Samir will be hanging on his elastic band.

Weight on elastic band (N)	Length of elastic band (cm)
0	
1	
2	
3	
4	
5	

This is what Samir will be measuring.

You must always put the units in.

This will be the length of the elastic band before Samir adds any weights.

Use a ruler to draw the straight lines in the table.

Emily's experiment

Emily did an experiment to find out how much of different substances would **dissolve** in water. This is the table she drew for her results.

There are no units here, because this column has the names of things.

These are the substances that Emily tested.

Substance	Number of scoops that dissolved in a glass of water
sugar	
salt	
Epsom salts	

There are no units here because the words already tell you how the substances were measured (in scoops).

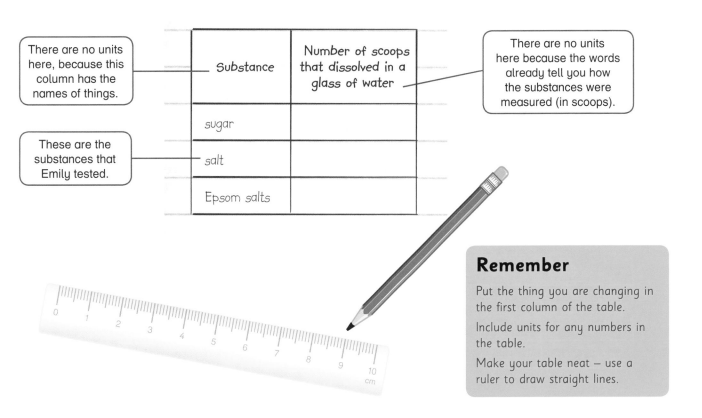

Remember

Put the thing you are changing in the first column of the table.

Include units for any numbers in the table.

Make your table neat – use a ruler to draw straight lines.

Bar charts

A bar chart is a way of showing your results. It can help you to see patterns in the results.

You can use a bar chart to show your results if one of the things you have studied can be described in words. If your results are two sets of numbers, you need to show your results using a line graph. You can find out more about line graphs on page 89.

Look at the two experiments described on page 87. Samir can use a line graph to show his results, because he has two sets of numbers in his table. Emily can use a bar chart to show her results because one of the things she studied can be described in words.

Emily's bar chart

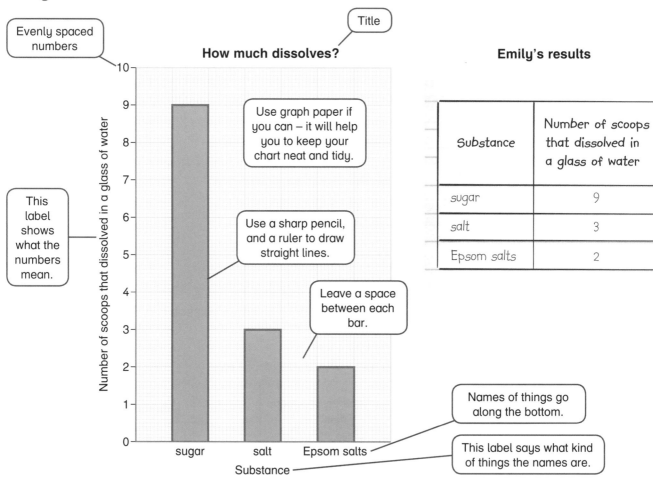

Emily's results

Substance	Number of scoops that dissolved in a glass of water
sugar	9
salt	3
Epsom salts	2

Test yourself

1. Draw a bar chart to show the results of Jacob's friction experiment (see page 85). The results are shown in the table below.

Jacob's results

Surface	Force needed (N)
polished	1
painted	3
rough wood	9

Remember

Use a bar chart to present your results when one of the things you have investigated can be described in words.

Line graphs

You can use a line graph to show your results when you have two sets of numbers.
Line graphs are useful because they can help you to make predictions.

Samir's line graph

These are Samir's results from his experiment on elastic bands (page 87).

This is the line graph that Samir drew to show his results.

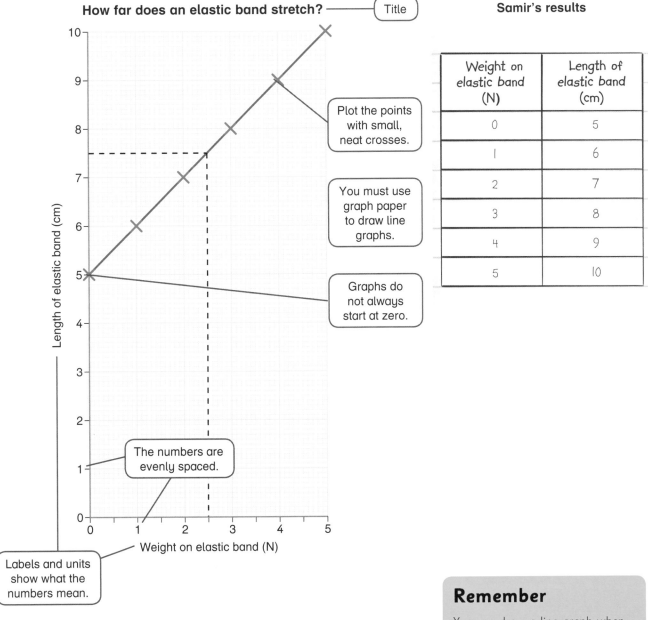

Samir's results

Weight on elastic band (N)	Length of elastic band (cm)
0	5
1	6
2	7
3	8
4	9
5	10

Using a line graph for predictions

Samir can use his line graph to predict how long the elastic band would
be if he hung a different **weight** on it. The dotted line on the graph shows
you how to use it to predict the length of the elastic band if Samir hangs
a 2.5N weight on it.

Remember

You can draw a line graph when
your results are two sets of
numbers.

Test yourself

1. Plot Samir's results (above)
   on a piece of graph paper.

Conclusions and evaluations

Conclusions

Your **conclusion** is what you have found out in an **investigation**. Before you write down your conclusion, you need to see if you can find any patterns in your results. It is usually easier to see patterns if you draw a bar chart or line graph to show your results.

Emily's conclusions

Look at the bar chart showing Emily's results. Emily's conclusion could be:

- 'Sugar dissolves the best.' ←—— *This is OK.*

- 'You can dissolve a lot more sugar in water than salt or Epsom salts.' ←—— *This is better, because it also mentions the other substances that Emily tested.*

- 'I can dissolve about three times as much sugar as salt in the same amount of water.' ←—— *This is even better, because Emily has said how much more sugar will dissolve.*

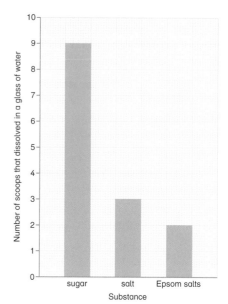

Samir's conclusions

Look at the line graph of Samir's results. Samir could make these conclusions:

- 'The elastic band is 10cm long when 5N is hanging from it.' ←—— *This is not very good – it is only saying what is in the table.*

- 'A big weight makes the elastic band long.' ←—— *This is better.*

- 'The bigger the weight, the longer the elastic band.' ←—— *This is best – always try to write your conclusion using comparing words (these are often words that end in 'er', for example smaller, shorter, heavier, lighter).*

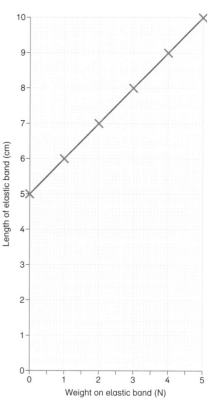

Evaluations

Your **evaluation** is where you say how good your results were or if you could do the investigation better if you had time to do it again. You should ask yourself these questions when you are evaluating your investigation.

- Did I do a **fair test**?
- Were my measuring instruments accurate enough?
- Have I got enough results?
- Do any of my results look wrong? Should I do any measurements again?

> **Remember**
>
> Your **conclusion** says what you found out in your **investigation**.
>
> Your **evaluation** says how good your results were.

Answers

Page 4
1 to make food
2 to support the plant and carry water
3 to hold the plant in the soil and to take in water
4 a plant A
  b It has more light to grow. (It will also grow well because it has more space to grow in a bigger plant pot.)

Page 5
1 water, air and light
2 water and nutrients
3 to make sure there are enough nutrients to keep plants healthy
4 They need deeper roots to support them in windy weather. A big plant also needs more water, so it needs bigger roots to take in water.
5 small, shallow roots, because grass plants are small

Page 6
1 Pollen is taken from one flower to another.
2 Pollen joins with an ovum.
3 Seeds are spread out away from the plant.
4 A new plant starts to grow from the seed.

Page 7
1 to attract insects
2 to attract insects
3 a seed
4 Pollination is when pollen travels between one flower and another. Fertilisation is when pollen that has already landed on a flower joins an ovum.

Page 8
1 so they get enough light, air, water, nutrients and space to grow
2 wind, water, animals or explosion
3 so they can be carried by the wind
4 so animals want to eat them

Page 9
1 carry water and support the plant
2 in little tubes inside the stem
3 You can see that the coloured water has only travelled up parts of the stem – these are the little tubes that Ruby talked about.
4 They are split up into smaller branches and spread out so they can get water from lots of soil. The spread out shape helps the roots to hold on to the soil.

Page 11
1 to make it easier to study them
2 Plants can make their own food, and animals cannot.
3 a Fulmar
  b Arctic tern
  c Lesser black-backed gull
  d Black-headed gull

Page 13
1 hair, produce milk, have live young
2 wet scales, lay eggs in water
3 six
4 No – the animals with eight legs are spiders, which do not have wings.

Page 15
1 The place where an organism lives.
2 a rabbit, squirrel, fox, owl, insects, worms, trees, grass, etc.
  b duck, fish, frog, dragonfly, kingfisher, heron, water lily, rushes, water boatman, etc.
3 Chemicals from farming can harm it; humans can help to keep it fit for many organisms to live there.
4 You would find worms, earwigs and woodlice. You would not find plants, because there is no light and plants need light to grow.

Page 17
1 any three from: birds, fish, reptiles, amphibians, insects
2 mammals, birds
3 amphibians
4 They are similar because they both lay eggs and the babies do not look like the adults at first. They are different because amphibians lay eggs in water and insects do not.

Page 19
1 pollen and ovum (egg)
2 sperm and eggs
3 asexual
4 They can reproduce even if there are no other plants to fertilise them.

Page 21
1 to grow, to stay healthy and for energy
2 meat, fish, milk, cheese, eggs, beans, lentils
3 bread, pasta, rice, cereals; milk, cheese, butter, oil, meat; sweets, cakes, biscuits, fizzy drinks
4 fruit and vegetables
5 It is a diet that gives your body all the things it needs in the right amounts.
6 She should eat more fruit and vegetables and more pasta, bread, etc., so she gets enough food for health and energy. She should not eat too much food containing fats and oils.

Page 22
1 to protect parts of your body, support you and let you move
2 protects the brain
3 It has joints, which let arms and legs bend.

Page 23
1 to move your bones
2 a A
  b It will relax and get longer.

Page 24
1 mouth
2 small intestine
3 mouth, stomach

Page 25
1 to cut and chew food
2 incisors, canines and molars
3 They are your first set of teeth.

Page 27
1 food, oxygen, water
2 heart
3 arteries
4 The number of heart beats per minute.
5 Your table should show 'low' for all the things that you do sitting down or lying down. It should show 'medium' for when you are standing up or walking around slowly and it should show 'high' when you are running around.

Page 29
1 baby, child, adolescent, adult
2 nine months
3 18
4 If you are a girl: breasts develop, hips get wider, hair starts to grow on the body, and your body changes so it is ready to have babies.
If you are a boy: voice gets lower, hair starts to grow on body and face, penis and testicles get larger, and your body changes so it is ready to start making babies.

Page 30
1 any two from: eat a balanced diet; exercise; do not take harmful drugs; keep your body clean
2 a substances that change the way your body works
  b something a drug does to you that you do not want
  c feeling sleepy after taking a medicine to stop you feeling travel sick
3 Alcohol can make you feel ill the next day and it can harm your body. Tobacco can damage your heart and lungs.
4 A driver who has been drinking could harm someone with their car. Non-smokers could breathe in the smoke from other people's cigarettes.

Page 31
1 lettuce
2 slug, thrush, sparrowhawk
3 slug, thrush
4 thrush, sparrowhawk
5 The arrows show the direction the food goes through the chain.

Page 32

1 It is the shape of a dead plant or animal preserved in rock.
2 It means that no animals or plants of that kind are alive any more.
3 Fossils from different times show animals have changed.

Page 33

1 any two ways, such as different coloured hair, different coloured eyes, shape of face, curliness of hair and so on
2 variation
3 any one from: taller, make bigger seeds, different flower colours
4 Some animals may run faster than others (or they may be taller/bigger or have slightly different coloured skin, scales or fur and so on).

Page 35

1 having special features that help animals and plants to survive in their habitat
2 large ears to listen for foxes, strong legs to run away
3 weather conditions change or new plants or animals arrive
4 tree trunks are paler as there is less pollution so the pale moths are hidden better (or so the dark moths are more likely to be seen and be eaten)

Page 37

1 **a** transparent and hard
  b brittle
2 It is absorbent and flexible.
3 It is strong and you can make it into different shapes.
4 Electricity cannot go through plastic.
5 It is flexible, so you can make it into clothes, and heat does not travel through it easily.

Page 38

1 She used the same size squares, and the same amount of water each time.

Page 39

1 degrees Celsius (or °C)
2 a thermometer
3 23°C

Page 40

1 metal
2 any two from: wood, plastic, foam, trapped air
3 There is lots of trapped air between the feathers, so a duvet is a good thermal insulator.

Page 41

1 any one from: plastic, rubber, wood
2 so electricity can flow through them
3 because electricity cannot flow through plastic, so you do not get a shock

Page 42

1 wood and metal (or anything else that is solid)

2 water and honey (or any other liquid)
3 any two from: sand, rice, flour, salt, sugar, etc.
4 any three from: hard, do not change shape, difficult to squash, volume does not change
5 any three from: runny, shape depends on the container it is in, hard to squash, volume does not change

Page 43

1 you can feel it when it is moving
2 oxygen, carbon dioxide, helium, natural gas (or any other gas)
3 You can squash a gas but you cannot squash a liquid. Gases spread out to fill a container, but liquids stay in the bottom of the container.
4 They change shape depending on the shape of the container they are in.

Page 44

1 solid, liquid and gas
2 cool it down to 0°C (freeze it)
3 a gas turning into a liquid
4 Evaporation happens at any temperature. Boiling only happens at 100°C.

Page 45

1 a liquid turning into a gas
2 spread out washing, so there is a bigger area for the water to evaporate from; heat the water (or clothes) to make the water evaporate faster; blow air over the clothes to carry away the evaporated water

Page 46

1 a gas turning into a liquid and the tiny drops of water formed on cold surfaces
2 There is a lot of water vapour in the air (which has evaporated from hot water in the sink or shower).
3 Water vapour in the air condenses on the cold can.
4 On a warm day, the water vapour does not cool down enough to condense.

Page 47

1 100°C
2 0°C
3 100°C

Page 49

1 the sea, lakes, rivers and plants
2 water vapour in the air condenses
3 It runs into rivers and lakes or soaks into the ground.
4 It is cleaned.
5 It runs into drains and is then treated at sewage works to make it safe before it is put back into rivers or the sea.
6 evaporating from the sea or a lake; condensing to make a cloud; freezing to make snow or hail; snow melting

Page 51

1 a container with lots of holes, which can be used to sort objects of different sizes
2 The sand will go through the holes but the peas will not because they are too big.
3 Water will go through tiny holes in the paper, but the grains of sand are trapped because they are too big to go through the holes.
4 The sugar dissolves and breaks into pieces that are small enough to fit through the holes in the filter paper.

Page 53

1 stir the water, use smaller pieces of sugar, use hot water
2 use more water
3 the same amount of sugar and the same kind of sugar each time; the same amount of water; she should have stirred them all in the same way

Page 54

1 The salt dissolves, so the pieces are small enough to go through the holes in the filter paper.
2 let the water evaporate
3 trap the evaporated water and make it condense again

Page 55

1 any three from: melting, dissolving, condensing, freezing, evaporating
2 irreversible

Page 57

1 concrete setting and bicarbonate of soda fizzing
2 A new material (ash) is formed.
3 You should have written down two of the safety rules on page 57.
4 The heat melts the wax. Some of the melted wax evaporates and some runs down the candle and becomes solid again. All these changes are reversible. Some of the wax burns and this is an irreversible change.

Page 59

1 They may be covered by soil and grass or by buildings or roads.
2 any two from: bricks, concrete, wood, etc.
3 It lasts a long time and it looks nice.
4 **a** water can run through something
  b drop water on it and see if the water soaks in
5 Granite, because it does not wear away. (Sandstone is also used in some places, even though it wears away easily, because it is easier to dig out of the ground.)

Page 60

1 decaying plants and animals
2 clay soils
3 sandy soils (or chalky soils)

Page 61

1 The shape of a dead plant or animal preserved in rock.
2 millions of years
3 The hard parts are more likely to last until they are turned into rock; the soft parts of animals are likely to be eaten.

Page 63

1 Transparent means 'see-through' and opaque means 'not see-through'.
2 The stick is opaque, so light cannot go through it. Light travels in straight lines, so it cannot bend around the stick.
3 The Earth is turning round on its axis and so the Sun seems to be in different places in the sky at different times of day.
4 a torch and two pieces of card
5 Move the screen closer to the torch or move the other card further away from the torch.

Page 65

1 because light travels in straight lines
2 They reflect light from car headlights better, so it is easier for the driver to see you.
3

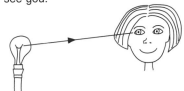

4 Your diagram should show the Sun, a car and you. There should be an arrow going from the Sun to the car, plus another arrow going from the car to your eyes.

Page 67

1 a the strings
  b the skin
2 how high or low a sound is
3 solids, liquids and gases
4 use soft materials such as carpets and curtains
5 to protect their ears from loud noises
6 Because they are so far away that they would not be able to hear each other (or the noise of the engines would be too loud if they just tried talking).

Page 69

1 blow harder
2 hit it gently
3 move the slider out to make the air column longer
4 Use a thicker string, a looser string or a longer string.

Page 70

1 a a sphere
  b any one from: photos from space; the bottom of ships disappear first when they sail away; ships can sail right around the world; shadows of the same object are different lengths in different places

2 Sun
3 Moon

Page 71

1 east
2 The Earth is spinning.
3 24 hours (or one day)
4 The shadow is long and to the west of the stick in the morning. It gets shorter until midday, when it points north, and then gets longer again during the afternoon and points further and further east.

Page 73

1 $365\frac{1}{4}$ days (or 1 year)
2 28 days
3 It reflects light from the Sun.
4 eight
5 A star is a light source (makes its own light) and a planet is not.

Page 75

1 a spring
2 newtons (N)
3 a force that slows down moving objects
4 have a smooth surface
5 give it a smooth shape
6 The tree has more area, so it has a larger air resistance.

Page 77

1 a force that pulls everything towards the Earth
2 the force of the Earth's gravity pulling on something
3 pulley, gear, lever
4 Choosing the right gear makes it easier to go up hills or choosing a different gear means you go faster.

Page 78

1 iron, steel (or any other magnetic material)
2 north pole and south pole
3 push away
4 north pole next to north pole or south pole next to south pole
5 Use a magnet to try to pick up the cans. The steel cans are the ones that the magnet will pick up.

Page 79

1 a any two from: TV, computer, washing machine (or anything else that you have to plug in)
  b Appliances need a lot of electricity.
2 torches, radio-controlled cars, mobile phones, etc.
3 The electricity they provide is not powerful enough to harm you.
4 You should have written out five of the rules on page 79.

Page 81

1 a Metals are good conductors of electricity.
  b Plastic is an insulator.
2 a There is no cell.
  b The circuit is not complete – it needs another wire.

c Both wires are connected to the same end of the cell.
d There is a gap in the circuit.

Page 82

1 A cell has a voltage written on it.
2 Put more bulbs in (or use a cell with a lower voltage).
3 The bulbs might break.
4 Put another cell in the circuit so there is more electricity or take a bulb out and join the wires up so the electricity does not have to be shared between the bulbs.

Page 83

1 It gets dimmer.
2 thick wire
3 dimmer
4 the length of the wire (and also the number of bulbs and cells)

Page 84

1

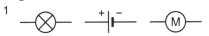

2 a closed switch
3

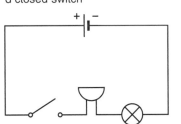

Page 85

1 A variable is something you can change in an investigation.
2 one
3 how much water it has, how much light it has, the temperature, the kind of soil, the size of pot

Page 86

1 a ruler
  b centimetres (cm) or millimetres (mm)
2 a measuring cylinder
  b cm^3 (or ml)

Page 88

1

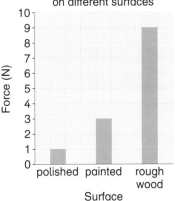

Force needed to pull a box on different surfaces

Page 89

1 Your graph should look like the one on page 89.

Glossary

adapted	having features to help an animal or plants survive
adolescent	a human changing from a child into an adult
amphibian	a **vertebrate** with moist skin that lays eggs in water
asexual reproduction	a way that plants (and some animals) reproduce. There is only one parent, and the offspring are identical to the parent.
bacteria	a type of **micro-organism**
balanced diet	a **diet** that contains the right amounts of all the **nutrients** you need
battery	two or more **cells** used together
bird	a **vertebrate** with feathers that lays eggs with hard shells
blood	red **liquid** that carries food around the bodies of humans and other animals
blood vessels	tubes that **blood** moves through (veins and arteries)
boiling	when a **liquid** is turning into a **gas** as fast as possible
burning	an **irreversible change** that gives out heat
canine teeth	pointed teeth that tear food
carnivore	an animal that eats only other animals
cell	part of a **circuit** that provides **electricity**
circuit	a complete loop for **electricity** to flow around
circulatory system	the **heart**, **blood vessels** and **blood**
components	parts of a **circuit**, such as **cells**, bulbs and switches
conclusion	what you have found out in an **investigation**
condensation	a **gas** turning into a **liquid** or the tiny drops of water that form on cold surfaces
conifers	trees that produce **seeds** in cones and have needle-shaped **leaves**
consumer	animals that eat plants or other animals
cuttings	small parts of a plant that can grow into new plants
day	the time when it is light because our part of the Earth is facing the Sun
decay	what happens when **micro-organisms** feed off dead organisms or off sugar and bits of food in your mouth and teeth
degrees Celsius (°C)	the units for measuring **temperature**
diet	the different foods that we eat
digestive system	the parts of your body that absorb food
disperse	spread out, as when **seeds** are dispersed from the parent plant
dissolve	break up into very tiny pieces (such as in water)
drug	a substance that changes the way your body works
electrical conductor	something that lets **electricity** flow through it
electrical insulator	something that does not let **electricity** flow through it
electricity	something that flows around a **circuit** and makes things such as TVs and light bulbs work
environment	the conditions in a **habitat**, including **temperature**, light, other organisms
evaluation	deciding how good your **investigation** was
evaporation	when a **liquid** changes into a **gas**
evolution	the way that types of living things change over time to adapt to their **environment**
extinct	when there are no more individuals of a particular kind of living thing
faeces	the waste part of food that has not been digested
fair test	an **investigation** where you only change one factor
fertilisation	when a **pollen** grain joins an **ovum** in a **flower**
fertiliser	a substance that adds **nutrients** to the **soil**
filter	paper with tiny holes in it that things such as sand cannot pass through
fish	a **vertebrate** with wet scales that lays eggs in water
flowering plants	plants that reproduce using **seeds**
flowers	the parts of a plant that help it to reproduce
food chain	a way of showing what eats what
forcemeter	an instrument containing a spring that is used to measure **forces**
forces	pushes or pulls
fossil	the shapes of dead plants or animals preserved in rocks

freeze	a **liquid** changing to a **solid**
friction	a **force** that slows down moving objects
fruit	something that surrounds **seeds**, which animals like to eat
function	the job something does
fungi	a type of **micro-organism**
gas	a substance that is invisible, easy to squash and spreads out to fill the container it is in
gear	wheels with teeth on the outside that are used to make moving things easier
germination	when **seeds** start to grow
gravity	a **force** that pulls everything towards the Earth
habitat	the place where an organism lives
heart	pumps **blood** around the bodies of humans and other animals
herbivore	an animal that only eats plants
incisors	the teeth at the front of the mouth that cut food into smaller pieces
inherit	to get things from your parents, such as your hair or eye colour
invertebrates	animals without backbones, including insects, worms and **molluscs**
investigation	finding an answer to a scientific question
irreversible change	a change that cannot be reversed, such as cooking food or **burning** wood
key	a diagram to help you to sort things into groups
large intestine	where water is removed from food
leaves	parts of a plant that make food using light, air and water
lever	a long pole that can be used to give a small **force** a greater effect
life cycle	the changes that happen to you as you get older
light source	something that gives out light, such as the Sun or a light bulb
liquid	a substance that is runny and cannot be squashed
magnet	something that can attract iron and can attract or **repel** another magnet
magnetic material	a material such as iron or steel that can be attracted by a **magnet**
mains electricity	powerful **electricity** that is supplied through sockets in the wall
mammal	a **vertebrate** that has hair, produces milk and has live young
melt	when a **solid** changes to a **liquid**
micro-habitat	a small **habitat**, such as under a stone or log
micro-organisms	tiny organisms, sometimes called microbes or germs
mixture	different things jumbled up together
molars	the teeth at the back of the mouth that grind up food
molluscs	**invertebrates** such as snails. Many molluscs have shells
mosses	a group of plants that do not have **flowers** or **roots**
muscles	parts of your body that move your bones
nectar	a sweet **liquid** that **flowers** make to attract insects
newtons (N)	the units used for measuring **force** and **weight**
night	when it is dark because our side of the Earth is facing away from the Sun
north pole	the name for one end of a **magnet**
nutrients	substances that plants need to keep healthy
nutrition	obtaining the substances the body needs from food
oesophagus	the tube that joins your mouth to your **stomach**
omnivore	an animal that eats plants and other animals
opaque	a material that light cannot travel through
orbit	the path that the Earth takes around the Sun or the Moon takes around the Earth
ovary	the part of a **flower** that contains the ova
ovum	one of the eggs that is in a **flower** (*plural*, ova)
permeable	allows **liquids** to pass through
petals	parts of a **flower** around the **stigma** – often brightly coloured to attract insects
photosynthesis	the process of making food in the **leaves** (using water, air and light)
pitch	how high or low a sound is
pollen	tiny grains made by the male parts of a **flower**

pollination	when **pollen** from one **flower** is taken to another flower
predator	an animal that kills other animals for food
prey	an animal that gets eaten by other animals
producer	any plant – plants make their own food from light, air and water
properties	what a material or substance is like
puberty	the stage in the human **life cycle** when children turn into adults
pulley	a rope that runs over small wheels that can be used to give a small **force** a greater effect
pulse	the movement of **blood** that you can feel in your neck or wrists
pulse rate	the number of **heart** beats per minute
rectum	where solid waste is stored before you go to the toilet
reflection	when light bounces off a material
repel	push away
reproduction	making new animals or plants
reptile	a **vertebrate** with dry scales that lays eggs with leathery shells
resistance, water and air	air resistance and water resistance are **forces** acting on objects moving through air or water that slow the object down
reversible change	a change that can be undone so the original **state** is restored, such as melting and freezing
roots	parts of a plant that hold it in the **soil** and take in water
saliva	a **liquid** produced in your mouth that is mixed with food
seeds	parts of a plant that can grow into new plants
sexual reproduction	**reproduction** that needs a male and a female parent
shadow	a place where there is no light because light cannot travel through **opaque** materials
skeleton	all the bones in your body
small intestine	where **nutrients** from food are moved into your **blood**
soil	material made from bits of rock and decaying organisms
solar system	the Sun and planets
solid	a substance that is usually hard, keeps the same shape and is difficult to squash
solution	a **mixture** of water with something dissolved in it
south pole	the name for one end of a **magnet**
sperm	produced by male animals as part of **sexual reproduction**
sphere	shaped like a ball
state	whether something is a **solid**, **liquid** or **gas**
stem	supports a plant and contains tubes to carry water up the plant
stigma	the top of the female part of a **flower**
stomach	where food is mixed with acid
style	the female part of a **flower** that joins the **ovary** to the **stigma**
temperature	how hot or cold something is
thermal conductor	something that lets heat flow through it
thermal insulator	something that does not let heat flow through it
thermometer	used to measure **temperature**
translucent	a material that light can go through, but you cannot see through it clearly
transparent	a material that light can travel through
trunk	the **stem** of a tree
variable	something that you can change in an **investigation**
variation	differences between individuals
vegetarian	someone who does not eat meat, but does eat eggs and things made from milk (such as cheese)
vertebrates	animals with backbones (vertebrates include **mammals**, **birds**, **fish**, **reptiles** and **amphibians**)
vibrate	move backwards and forwards quickly
water cycle	the cycle of **evaporation** and **condensation** that moves water from the sea or lakes into the air, where it falls again as rain and runs back into the sea
water vapour	water when it is a **gas**
weight	the **force** of **gravity** pulling on something
year	the length of time it takes for the Earth to go around the Sun once